CHINA JOURNAL

Other Books by Robert Lee

FAITH AND THE PROSPECTS OF ECONOMIC COLLAPSE (John Knox Press)
THE SOCIAL SOURCES OF CHURCH UNITY — Selected for the Kennedy White
House Library (Abingdon)
CITIES AND CHURCHES, Editor (Westminster)
PROTESTANT CHURCHES IN THE BROOKLYN HEIGHTS (New York Protestant
Council)
RELIGION AND SOCIAL CONFLICT (Editor with Martin Marty (Oxford
University Press)
RELIGION AND LEISURE IN AMERICA (Abingdon)
THE CHURCHES AND THE EXPLODING METROPOLIS, Editor (John Knox Press)
DIRECTOR OF CENTERS FOR THE STUDY OF SOCIETY (Towne House
Publishers)
STRANGER IN THE LAND: A STUDY OF THE CHURCH IN JAPAN (Lutterworth;
Friendship)
THE SCHIZOPHRENIC CHURCH (Westminster)
THE PROMISE OF BENNETT (Lippincott)
THE SPOUSE GAP, with Marjorie Casebier (Abingdon; Collins; Friedrich Bahn
Verlag, Konstanz)
MARRIAGE ENRICHMENT SHARING SESSIONS (Minister's Life Resources)

Contributing Author

THE CHURCH AND ITS CHANGING MINISTRY (General Assembly, United
Presbyterian Church)
THE DILEMMA OF ORGANIZATIONAL SOCIETY (E. P. Dutton)
EVANGELISM AND CONTEMPORARY ISSUES (Tidings)
THE CHALLENGE TO REUNION (McGraw-Hill)
HEIRLOOMS (Harper and Row)
DICTIONARY OF CHRISTIAN ETHICS (Westminster Press)
MASTERPIECES OF CHRISTIAN LITERATURE (Salem Press)
ETHICS AND BIGNESS (Harper and Brothers)
PREACHING ON NATIONAL HOLIDAYS (Fortress Press)
THE CHURCH AND URBAN RENEWAL (Lippincott)
LIFE AND MISSION OF THE CHURCH (National Student Christian Federation)
CHRISTIANISME SOCIAL (Coopérative d'Éditions et de Publications, Paris)

CHINA JOURNAL

Glimpses of a Nation in Transition

by

ROBERT LEE

With the aid of the Lee family:
May, Mellanie, Marcus
Matthew, Wendy, Michele

Photographs by Matt Lee

EAST/WEST PUBLISHING COMPANY
San Francisco

Book designed and typesetted by William Rock.
Cover designed by Walter Leong.
East/West book project coordinated by Cecilia Eng, and assisted by Mary
Castagnozzi and Cho-yip Lau.

Library of Congress catalog card number : 80-52783
ISBN: 0-934-78800-6

Published by East/West Publishing Company
838 Grant Avenue
San Francisco, California 94108

First printing 1980

This book is dedicated to
the friendship
between the Chinese
and American peoples

Contents

Visit to a Nanjing Primary School • More Notes on the
Cultural Revolution • Notes on Sexist Language and
Women's Lib

Preface

A new wind is blowing in the East! Not the militant gale that threatens to overpower and prevail, but rather the fresh breeze that comes with the opening of doors and windows, bringing with it the promise of change.

Something new and exciting is stirring in the air! China has opened its doors to welcome travelers—one hundred thousand of them in 1978 (not counting those from Hong Kong and Macao), equal to the total number for the past twenty-three years. Three-quarters of a million in 1979, and even more visitors are expected in the immediate future, for fascination grows about this most populous and oldest country in the world. This time China has a renewed sense of dignity, for its doors are being opened from within and not by pressure or force from foreign powers.

The road leading to China has been a well-traveled route going back before the birth of Christ to the days of the "Silk Road" that linked the "Central Kingdom" to the Roman Empire. In ancient times, august representatives of imperial courts, merchants, traders, and fortune hunters came calling. In recent centuries, many foreigners have ventured to China with military or commercial conquest in mind and have unshielded their avaricious instincts.

By comparison, the Lee family trip is a modest and personal odyssey—to enrich our own understanding of the land of our forefathers. As fourth and now fifth generation Chinese-Americans, our family has felt quite severed from our ethnic roots—at a time when the search for ethnic identity has become meaningful.

At the earliest opportunity, which coincided with my sabbatical leave, we joined an Overseas Chinese tour group consisting of sixteen persons. My wife, May, and I, along with our five children (Marcus, Mellanie, Matthew, Wendy, and Michele), and May's sister, Bettie, spent a month during parts of November and December, 1979, traveling to ten major cities and some smaller village areas in China. The cities we visited were: Guangzhou (Canton), Xi'an (Sian), Taiyuan, Shijiazhuang (Shihchiachuang), Beijing (Peking), Nanjing (Nanking), Wuxi (Wushih), Shanghai, Hangzhou (Hangchow), and Guilin (Kweilin).

Early in our travels, I was struck with the idea that although China is an ancient civilization, it is only thirty years young in its new metamorphosis, and it is still caught up in revolutionary changes. Indeed, it is going through a period of transitional turbulence. One could not expect otherwise. Prior to Chairman Mao Zedong's death on September 10, 1976, a China without Mao was hardly thinkable. All sorts of chaotic discord and dismantling of a nation were predicted by China watchers, once Mao's massive presence was removed from the scene.

Recall also that the wise and steadying influence of Zhou Enlai was gone with his death at the beginning of the same year that Mao died. It's a wonder that more turmoil and tumult did not ensue with the demise of these two venerable architects of the People's Republic of China.

Yet, just two years later, China is on a new road, opening up its doors to fresh influences. Following normalization of relationships, formal diplomatic ties between the People's Republic of China and the United States were resumed on January 1, 1979, with embassies opening on March 1. Now American tourists and business leaders (as well as foreigners from other lands) are flocking to China in large numbers. This tide is likely to swell, as new hotel accommodations are rapidly under construction, and English-speaking guides are being trained to meet the anticipated need. Moreover, in these inflationary times, the Chinese government is considering a general reduction in prices for these visits.

Since our Overseas Chinese tour group was diverse in age and occupations (from age 14 to 75, from computer scientist to cook), we visited a wide assortment of things, such as museums, factories, agricultural communes, temples, recreational centers, schools, nurseries, markets, homes, and archaeological digs. Had we been a medical, mental health, farming, or educational group, more specific focus would have been given to these interests, as we learned in encountering such groups in the various hotels where we stayed. Since four persons in our group spoke and read Mandarin fluently, and an equal number spoke Cantonese, they were generous in interpreting to the rest of us. We wish to thank John Wong, York and Jeanne Frank, and Gloria Heung; also Frank and Mary Mar, Warren Quock, and Myron and Mary Lum.

On the matter of language translation, I was impressed and grateful for all the assistance we received. China Travel Service provided a guide who met us in Guangzhou and stayed with us throughout the trip. Since ours was an Overseas Chinese group, he spoke Mandarin and Cantonese. However, in each city we visited, we were escorted by an English-speaking guide. Then at particular sites, such as museums, temples, tombs, and archaeological digs, there would be an additional guide who would speak in the language of the group—be it English, Japanese, French or German. I found this service much more accommodating than in European countries we have visited. The Chinese seem to bend over backwards to render all possible aid and assistance.

China, of course, is filled with rich and dazzling relics from its past eras of high civilization. One could easily become totally immersed in its past glories. At the same time, China's current developments are so startling that one could become utterly fascinated with present-day realities. In a way the contemporary changes are perhaps more decisive than the persisting strands of continuity. I trust that this journal places equal emphasis on both past and present.

Everywhere we went, we sought out persons with whom to converse on an individual basis, and individuals also approached us. Hence our experiences and insights were not altogether "pre-packaged." Indeed, we were on guard against a "canned" exposure, and therefore made liberal requests to see particular facets of life, which were generally honored, given the constraints of time and distance.

Obviously a month's travel in a nation so vast and complex hardly qualifies one to be an expert. It should only reveal how little one knows and help to formulate better questions for the next visit. The observations in this journal are strictly personal and individualized reflections, notes to myself, made on the spur of the moment, and entered into my notebook in the wee hours, after a long day's journey. As befits a journal, another scribbler might perceive other saliencies or interpret similar events differently.

Our family returned from this trip brimming with pride in China's cultural achievements in the past and present. We caught the sense of excitement, of a freshness and openness of spirit in the air. We took pride in the attitude of self-determination after over a century of humiliation by foreign powers. We were fascinated by the changes. It felt as if we were watching a rose bud, closed for so long, suddenly opening up before our eyes, to reveal new beauties. We sensed the refreshing dynamism of a new day, which is so fraught with risk and promise. We were always dimly aware of the high achievements and splendors of the past. However, now we have seen and can identify more intimately with these great achievements of the human spirit.

China Journal was initially written for myself and for our family to share. If it should serve a useful purpose for a wider readership, that would be delightful. Come join us on our journey!

This journal begins at the railway station in Hong Kong, as we are about to board the train that routes directly from Hong Kong to Guangzhou (Canton).

*
* *

I

From Hong Kong to Guangzhou (Canton)

November 11, 1979

At the train station in Kowloon, we encountered an unbelievable mass of humanity, burdened with packages of all shapes and sizes. Here were teeming hordes of people, who were waiting to catch the train to Guangzhou (Canton). No longer does the train stop at a checkpoint just across the border; now it goes straight through to Guangzhou where all the customs formalities are handled.

Crowds of people press in upon us, so that it is virtually impossible to keep our small group together as a unit, despite the valiant effort of our tour leader in waving her small, yellow banner to keep the flock from straying. As we all surge towards the gate, awaiting the signal to board the train, I turn to my fellow traveler, Frank Mar, pastor of the Chinese Presbyterian Church in Oakland, California, and jestingly remark: "Now I understand why the white people in California were so horrified by the threat of an invading 'yellow horde.'" Frank agreed and noted that in Oakland during the mid-1850s one out of every seven persons was Chinese. The mass of humanity was simply overwhelming, as we moved with the tides toward the gates.

Excitement permeated the air, for the time of departure was imminent. A Western newspaper reporter standing behind us overheard our conversation. Tapping my shoulder, he expressed surprise at the quality of the spoken English he had heard. We immediately struck up a conversation. As a correspondent stationed in Beijing, he had gone to Guangzhou to cover a news event—Bjorn Borg's tennis exhibition. He readily confessed that this was just a pretext for visiting Hong Kong for much-needed "rest and recreation." When queried about Beijing and China in general, to my utter surprise, he expressed a negative assessment. When pressed for examples, he cited the dull, dirty, and drab appearance of Beijing, noting the ugly scenes ("Tiananmen Square is just

1

an ugly Russian import."). He particularly stressed the oppressive political climate in which he claims "freedom is a joke."

Since I learned he speaks little or no Chinese, I asked about his sources of information. He replied that he draws from a "network of informants" who contact him, or arrange to meet him in public places, or tip him off to things that are happening. Wow—shades of Washington, D.C.'s mysterious "Deep Throat," I thought to myself; had this non-American correspondent gotten too enamored with the Bernstein and Woodward style of reporting?

He continued in a cautionary vein: "Things are not what they appear to be; most visitors don't stay long enough to get a close, hard look." He was pleased to hear that I would be spending a month in China, for in that time I should be able to obtain a more accurate picture.

Now that the gates were opened, our conversation continued on the run. By now I was dismayed and stunned; my emotions had run the gamut from exhilaration to apprehension. My daughter Mellanie broke into the conversation to ask bluntly: "If you don't like it in China, why do you stay there?" His reply: "It's a great place for a newspaper correspondent, because this is where the action is, where the news is breaking out!"

I must confess that this first encounter with a foreign correspondent from Beijing left me emotionally shaken. Only later was I able to regain my composure and remind myself that I have come to China to let the experience speak to me in a fresh way. I had made up my mind not to carry the excess baggage of preconceptions, not to be weighed down by grandiose or pretentious plans to unveil the "mysterious East" or to penetrate the "inscrutable," but simply to respond to what I see, hear, and feel. Besides, I remembered an earlier tour group which May and I joined to visit the great European cities. One couple was always complaining and nagging about how each of the cities we visited could not stack up to Ventura, California (of all places!). Tiring of their nattering negativism, I finally turned to them in Paris and remarked, "Why don't you quit looking at the turds and look at the towers?"

On the Way to Guangzhou

Pouring through the gates, we reached our reserved seats on the train and settled down for the long ride. Guangzhou is about 113 miles away. I am glad we are going by train, for this affords a good opportunity to see the countryside. We passed through endless miles of lush, fertile land and rice paddies in this productive agricultural region of south China. Also, sugar cane, peanuts, corn, cabbage, beans, and other fruits and vegetables were growing.

The fields were carefully tilled in both the flat lands and the terraced hilly areas. We could see how every bit of cultivable space is used, for despite its vast geographical size, only a small proportion of China's land is arable. The land is well irrigated with a network of canals and ditches, although now and again we see women transporting water with the aid of the shoulder-pole. Today is Sunday, but it is simply another working day for these tillers of the soil.

Reforestation is everywhere in view as slim pine trees of different heights are growing on the hills that border the farmland in order to prevent erosion. When our train passes, the workers pause, wave, smile, and some even clap their hands. Rarely did we see any sighs of mechanization; only now and again there was a tractor in the field or a home-made, old-fashioned, engine-powered contraption used for hauling. Basically, what we saw was lots of man-power and woman-power, aided by water buffalo. Indeed, if the "Wealth of Nations" (Adam Smith) resides in its people power, then China excels. Manual labor is surely not held in contempt. It is this spirit of work, this mystical equation of work with reality, that led Mao to foment his daring revolution, not in the industrial cities, but in China's countryside among the peasantry. Mao's creation of agricultural communes stirred the peasants to new productive efforts. By dint of hard labor, men and women literally have moved mountains to develop more arable land.

My guess is that full-scale mechanization of agriculture will not find root here in this labor-intensive society; but surely Schumacher's notion of appropriate, intermediate technology in *Small Is Beautiful* would find a congenial home and contribute to the modernization thrust of agriculture.

As we passed along the route, we busily pointed out interesting sights to one another: a gaggle of geese; an old, weather-beaten woman tending her ducks; a lovely grove of bamboo; a village, where the children and their parents gathered to wave at us; a brick factory; a village that looked quite modern and progressive; another village that seemed backward and primitive; women washing laundry in a stream; a man on a bicycle conveying a load appropriate for a Bekins truck; boys cavorting or fishing in a pond; just people, working, and living, and playing—like people everywhere in the world, content when they can enjoy a good harvest.

Our reverie is broken as a vendor pushes a cart filled with food up the aisle and shouts out her fare. A dish of rice, vegetables, chicken or beef costs $1.25. By now, we have worked up an appetite and can down the tasty food—even the unaccustomed liver and gizzard of the chicken, which are cooked in the rice.

Up and down the aisle of the speeding train, an attendant was constantly sweeping and mopping the floor and fussily cleaning up after us. I told our children she was the original immaculate conception. She was a young women in her late teens with a compulsion for cleanliness and a bland, bored expression on her face. She gave me a stony stare for spilling some cake crumbs on the floor, as if to remark, "You stupid idiot, I just cleaned that floor."

Arrival

At Guangzhou, we disembarked from the train into another mob scene. The station platform was filled with people who were carrying unbelievable loads from the outside world into China. A quick sighting indicated that the baggage and boxes contained largely consumer goods—such as TV sets, stereos, cameras, tape recorders, radios, cotton and other fabrics, even sewing machines and the ubiquitous but highly valued bicycle. Apparently many of these people are kinfolks from Hong Kong bringing high-ticket items to their relatives in China. There must be a craving for consumer goods manufactured in the capitalist countries. I can't help wondering whether the invasion of luxury items sets people apart, makes for new class distinctions based on material privileges, or otherwise creates resentment or invidiousness. I can well imagine the duty that must be paid at the customs desk!

Bearing no such material burdens, our tour group—designated Number 446—was whisked away by two guides from China Travel Service and cleared customs quickly—without bothering to open any of our luggage. This was the first of many subsequent indications of the preferential treatment accorded to U.S. citizens. The red carpet has been unfurled for Americans.

Extra precautions, however, are taken for residents of Hong Kong and Macao. Doubtless, there are good reasons for this, for the traffic in smuggling in goods for resale in the black market is extremely lucrative. For example, a TV set may cost US$400 in Hong Kong, plus an additional charge of $400 for duty at the customs desk. However, if sold on the black market, that same set could command a price of 3,000 U.S. dollars! Profits of that magnitude are bound to challenge the venturesome capitalist from Hong Kong, relative or not. I wonder how many people commute from Hong Kong to "visit their relatives"!

Moving along from the train station to board the special bus, we can feel the hot and humid Guangzhou weather. After exchanging greetings, welcoming speeches, and a round of applause, we are informed that the Canton Trade Fair is under way, the city is deluged with tourists, and our hotel room, which had previously been reserved, is now occupied by others. Horrors! Some of us recall reading about the mess created by the Trade Fair the previous year. So many Westerners attended the Fair and hotel accommodations were so overbooked that people were sleeping in the hallways and lobbies. Some irate Americans, accustomed to fancier sleeping quarters, simply turned around and went home.

What to do? Not to worry, said our guides, who apologetically and graciously suggested that we all have dinner at the Overseas Chinese hotel and they would try their best to resolve the problem. Into the dining room we trooped with our carry-on luggage encircling our table.

Since this was to be our very first sit-down meal in China, we were all wondering and speculating about the dishes we would be served. However, everything that came was what we were accustomed to in Cantonese food, with one exception: water buffalo meat cooked with green (bok choy) vegetables. Although our family made frequent table jokes about being served such specialties as dog, snake, or monkey brains, we never did taste these delicacies either here or elsewhere in China. Nevertheless, my son Marcus kept alive this tease, which he delighted in directing at one of my more squeamish daughters.

Before our tasty, eight-course dinner had ended, our guides came smilingly to our tables with the happy news of a solution. We would have to board the bus and drive north for three hours to a hot springs resort community, where space was available for our party.

What a delightful surprise when we arrived at the Tsung Hua Hot Springs. It was a lovely health spa located in a beautifully tended garden setting, a resort where VIPs and their guests came for relaxation. What a welcomed relief after that long train ride and bumpy bus trip. Walking through the gardens, we could smell the fresh country air and the fragrant jasmine blossoms. We admired the trash bins scattered along the walkways, for they were made of green ceramic and had a precious antique look that made them seem inappropriate as garbage receptacles. In the center was a large, clear lake with warm mineral water still available. Surrounding the lake were exquisite gardens and bamboo groves. The chrysanthemums were in full bloom. I have never seen such beauty and artistry, for here were many examples of three hundred or more flowers all springing from a single chrysanthemum stock. What a commentary on the idea of one body and many branches. Bamboo and chrysanthemums and tranquil hills—what an idyllic setting for poets and artists.

As one might expect from such a luxurious place, our rooms were elegant. Actually they were suites. In addition to the large bedroom, there was an outer, enclosed patio area overlooking the garden and lake. A huge bathroom came complete with a Japanese-style sunken bathtub which could be filled with natural hot spring mineral water. Each room had a large mosquito net dangling from the high ceiling. When my daughter Wendy first caught sight of this suspended net, it startled her until she found out its intended usage.

After a restful night's sleep and a hearty breakfast, the next morning we took a leisurely stroll around the gardens and the lake. Suddenly, we crossed a bridge, saw a small village within walking distance, and entered into another world.

Whereas the resort was luxurious, the small, village commune we wandered into was just above the level of subsistence. The village was situated around a large rice paddy. About 125 families worked the rice field and also grew corn and other vegetables. They lived in buildings that were run-down or crumbling. Here and there, new buildings of brick adobe were being constructed. Walking through the village, we noted that half a dozen older women were taking care of the babies in a hallway that opened up to the other homes. This facility constituted the nursery school. The fact that there was no regular nursery-school meeting room is indicative of the relative impoverishment of this commune. We came upon an old building with two posters tacked on the wall. One told about rules and regulations of coupon rationing. The other gave specific instructions on family planning and birth control. It listed various incentives and rewards for having fewer children and stressed responsibility for limiting birth through abortion, sterilization, and birth control devices.

As we were reading the posters, a man came out from a nearby room and invited us into his office. It was the commune brigade's office and he was the leader. He told us about the commune, its production plans and schedule, and cheerfully answered our questions. The walls of his office were filled with graphs and charts indicating progress and production according to work teams. These charts were designed to spur competition by ranking each team's output. The leader explained that commune members not only work in the commune's field, but they may also grow their own products in their privately owned parcel of land and sell these products for their own private gain.

Next we visited the commune's elementary school and joined the children in their recess period. Our presence excited them as they playfully gathered around and exchanged greetings. We noted that the school rooms were very spartan and teaching materials seemed scant. The large, open-air, concrete gymnasium looked like a bombed-out wreck because that's precisely what happened. It had not been repaired from the old days of the Japanese bombing. We took polaroid pictures of many of the children for them to keep. By now it was time to walk back to our rooms, repack and take the bus back to Guangzhou. However, we were all glad to see this contrast between the luxurious resort and the barren, backward small village nearby.

Having left our hot springs resort, we returned to the city center where our accommodations were ready. Guangzhou is a large city of five million people (consisting of the city of 1.6 million, and six rural counties), and is situated in South China on the Pearl River. Its climate is like Miami or Southern California. Later we were to experience the sudden shift of moving from the warmth of Guangzhou to the chilly and freezing climate of North China. For over twenty-two hundred years, Guangzhou has been an important trading port with the outside world. These contacts have given this city the reputation of being a center for innovation. Indeed, this city has been hospitable to revolutionary movements and ideas.

The people of Guangzhou have been imbued with an independent spirit. They speak their mind. It was they who resisted and rose up against the British in a disgraceful war in which the British forced the

Chinese to purchase their cargoes of opium in return for tea and silver. It was these Cantonese people, fighting heroically with bamboo poles, who chased away the British troops who were armed with rifles and modern weapons. Finally the British returned with reinforcements and heavier armaments to achieve conquest.

Over the years, Guangzhou has produced many martyrs. Therefore, it was no accident that our first visit was to the Memorial for 72 Martyrs of Sun Yat-sen's revolution against the Manchu dynasty. Overseas Chinese in communities all over the world contributed funds to build this memorial as a way of saying that those who died during the ill-fated revolutionary uprising on April 27, 1911 did not lose their lives in vain. Known also as the "Yellow Flower Park" because all the beautiful flowers grown here come in shades of yellow, the Mausoleum of the 72 Martyrs is a sort of twin to another Memorial Garden to the Martyrs in the Guangzhou Uprising on December 11, 1927. Some five thousand revolutionaries are buried here in this garden, which is also known as the "Red Flower Park" because of its red flowers. In viewing all the yellow and red beauties of nature, I felt they bore no resemblance to a yellow or red peril—both dreaded American images.

When one considers the Cantonese resistance to the British during the Opium Wars and all those who gave their lives in following Sun Yat-sen, Mao Zedong and Zhou Enlai, one senses how important Guangzhou has been in modern China's political history.

Being here on the soil of Guangzhou gave me a sense of pride. I confess that all my life, I've been rather apologetic about my Cantonese background, believing that we Cantonese from southern China were an inferior breed to the educated, taller, proud folks from northern China. After all, our forefathers were lower class, unskilled, uneducated, illiterate, coolie laborers who went to America. In the new "Land of the Golden Mountain," they were in turn rejected and kicked around and demoted to the most menial forms of employment. I learned that far from being servile, the Cantonese have been in the forefront of revolutionary changes. I realized that it was this spirit of innovation, this adventuresome spirit of risk-taking, that enabled Cantonese immigrants to journey to America. Perhaps Guangzhou, more than any other place in China is the crucible for keeping alive the spirit of independence. I felt proud of my Cantonese roots.

Despite Guangzhou's warm climate and plentiful rainfall favoring crops, for centuries the fields lacked proper irrigation and were periodically subject to drought, flood, typhoon, and insect pests. Cantonese people have suffered through extended periods of famine and poverty. It was during one of these depressing periods that my great-grandfather pulled up stakes for the journey to America. Even from our hotel window near the center of the city, we could gaze out and watch workers tilling the soil and harvesting the crops. It has been an excellent year for the farmers. I couldn't help wondering: were it not for the drought and famine over a century and a quarter ago, might not one of those tillers of the soil out there be me!

November 12. Acrobatic Show

This evening we spent a delightful and entertaining time at what was to be the first of many acrobatic shows, an art form which dates back two thousand years. Our show this evening featured gymnastics, spectacular stunts, balancing acts, juggling, magic, dances, roller skaters, ventriloquists, clowns, and slapstick comedy. The show was held in a large stadium for a capacity crowd of perhaps twenty thousand.

As I looked around the audience, it seemed to consist mainly of peasants and workers with their families. I learned that most of the workers and peasants received free passes, which were distributed through their communes or factories. The price of admission (seven cents) was what I would regard as ridiculously low for such a splendid show.

We all felt that the performers were excellent. They combined skill with spontaneity and expressed a joy and flair for their work. We foreigners sat together in the best seats of the house and started to applaud each act. To our surprise we were the only ones applauding individual acts. In China, one waits until the end when there is general clapping from both audience and performers.

One other surprise that took a while for my backside to recover from was that the entire show lasted two and one-half hours without any interruption. This experience, so early in the trip, helped me to develop endurance and also taught me not to drink too much liquid before performances.

November 13. More Sights to See

By now, I'm beginning to fall into the routine. Up by 6:30 or 7:00 a.m. for a quick stroll on our own; breakfast at 7:30; meet at the bus by 8:15 or 8:30 and away we go. This morning our bus takes us up a long, winding, narrow road to White Cloud Mountain, where we have a commanding view of the entire region. On the way up, we pass by hundreds of school children who take the ascent on foot. All along the way the children wave at us and do not seem to resent the fact that we are riding and they are hiking.

We finally reach the top of the mountain on a clear, warm day and can see all of Guangzhou and its environs. From this vantage point, we can see how the urban landscape blends with the rural areas, how some factories and small industries are visible in the countryside and how vegetation is growing in urban spaces. Smokestacks belching dark smoke into the clear atmosphere give telltale signs of the pollution problem, which will likely become more serious.

White Cloud Mountain covers an extensive area which is filled with hiking paths that lead to one picturesque pavilion after another. Many of them are named as rendezvous points for lovers. Here we learned that the Chinese are very concrete in the way places are named. This place is called White Cloud Mountain because here is where one can reach out and touch the clouds. On this day, no clouds are visible, but many fountains, rock grottoes, and well-tended gardens may be enjoyed.

Our leisurely stroll brings us to a teahouse, where we rest and sip hot tea, while our guide spins one yarn after another, each relating to White Cloud Mountain. Apparently many fables about this place have been transmitted orally through the centuries. In these pages I will resist the temptation to tell these stories and relate only one: Once upon a time, a very tyrannical emperor lived in these parts. In his quest for immortality, he summoned a prominent doctor to his court and commanded that this physician find the fountain of youth, which was said to be located at White Cloud Mountain, so that the emperor could live forever. The doctor was granted three days. Failure in this mission meant a fate of certain death by beheading. Working furiously, the doctor found the fountain of youth on the side of a cliff. Now he was faced with a dilemma: If he were to tell the emperor about the rejuvenating waters, this terrible ruler would perpetuate his reign of terror. If he did not report success, he would be killed. His choice was to jump over the cliff, taking his own life and thus sparing the people from continued oppression. Our guide reported that this is an ancient fable, transmitted for generations. However, I thought how curious it was that this legend fitted perfectly the spirit of the present-day slogan: "Serve the People."

Descending from our mountain-top experience, we visited another beautiful site—Guangzhou's chrysanthemum gardens. I have never seen such a profusion of exquisitely tended flowers. It seemed unbelievable that as many as three thousand blossoms could emanate from just two chrysanthemum stocks. A number of the chrysanthemum plants we saw had over a hundred flowers growing from one stock. I wondered to myself if this is what Chairman Mao had in mind when he enunciated the "Let a Hundred Flowers Bloom" campaign, which then was abruptly ended. Perhaps Mao did see a "hundred flowers," but was shocked and surprised to find so many different stocks. Therefore he grew intolerant and ordered a clampdown. I wonder if this chrysanthemum garden doesn't provide us with a clue about the alternations between freedom and control over the past three decades. Do the flowers all have to be red?

In the same garden of beauty was a ghastly symbol—a red pavilion where Chiang Kai-shek's Kuomintang forces beheaded communists who had been captured. This pavilion is a brutal reminder of the struggles between the two contending political parties here in Guangzhou. It was said that the KMT conducted these public executions here to serve as an object lesson to the people.

Seeing all these chrysanthemums in bloom, I was reminded of an earlier childhood experience. I recalled that during the Depression years, our entire family of eight children and parents worked in the chrysanthemum fields of San Mateo and Palo Alto, California. Apparently the skill of growing these flowers was transferred from Guangzhou to California. Our family used to bend way over to pick the tiny ears off the growing plant so that a single, sturdy stock could develop and form a beautiful flower. Later in life I saw how many of these flowers ended up in the hands of co-eds, who waved them from the rooting section during the Stanford University football games.

Our next stop was a visit to a celebrated place—the National Institute of the Peasants' Movement. In 1926 Mao Zedong had been the head-master of this school and Zhou Enlai had taught here. It was begun in 1924 as a training center for the revolution. Three hundred twenty-seven trainees were recruited from twenty-seven provinces throughout China. After their training, they returned to their respective locales to foment and organize the revolution. The Institute's curriculum consisted of twenty-five courses. Mao himself taught three courses, including "Prob-lems Facing Peasants" and "Education of Farmers in the Countryside." Zhou taught military science and agricultural subjects. Trainees were required to do field work by going to the rural areas and learning the problems of the peasants firsthand. An effort was made to integrate the-ory with practice. Besides military training, the curriculum also in-cluded painting, singing, history, and physical education.

Although burned down and destroyed by the KMT, the Peasants' In-stitute was restored after Liberation. We were taken on a tour of its facil-ities, including the classrooms, library, mess hall, dormitories, gymna-sium, and the inevitable rooms where Chairman Mao and Zhou slept. In one room was a large map showing the number of students coming from particular provinces. Not surprisingly, Guangdong (the province of which Guangzhou is the capital) had the largest number—42 recruits out of a total of 327.

In the mess hall, four large pictures were hung on the walls—Marx, Engels and Lenin on one side, and Sun Yat Sen on the other. Later on in the trip we were to see a frequent foursome, whose pictures hung on the wall: Marx, Engels, Lenin and Stalin. Of course, Mao's picture is ubiqui-tous, and Chairman Hua is gaining in public exposure. The picture of Stalin puzzled me, since he is held in such low esteem in the United States. China's quarrel is not primarily with Stalin but with Khrushchev. Whereas Stalin rendered technical aid during a "honeymoon" period, Khrushchev began criticizing Mao and his development of Chinese com-munes as "reactionary." In July, 1960, at a critical moment when China was being plagued by droughts and then floods, and was suffering from economic privations, Khrushchev abruptly withdrew Soviet experts who were working on engineering and scientific projects. He also rescinded contracts to supply machinery, gas and oil. Recall that when Khrushchev assumed power he began a campaign to expose Stalin as a ruthless "per-secutor," "bandit," "idiot," and "fool." The Chinese responded by saying that although Stalin made mistakes, the attack on him was unfair. This infuriated Khrushchev, who sought to assert superiority over China and other Communist nations. Incidents along the Sino-Soviet border began. China felt betrayed by Khrushchev. Possibly as a needle to stick at Khru-shchev, China continued to carry its portraits of Stalin, with whom there had been no essential beef.

This has already been a long day, but would you believe there is yet another site to visit? The Guangzhou Museum is located in the city's oldest building—a five-story pagoda-like tower which dates from the 14th century. Each story contains artifacts from a different period of Chinese history. We climb five flights of stairs to the top to see the earliest period and then work our way down to modernity. As one might imagine, all the inventions and profiles of their inventors are on display: paper, printing, the abacus, gunpowder, silk, porcelain, paper currency, canal locks, and the compass. When one gazes at the various contributions to civilization that have been made by China, one has some understanding of why the Chinese regarded outsiders as inferior barbarians and became insular. Perhaps by shutting off the rest of the world centuries ago, China is now having to play catch-up, for in a world of change, to stay put is to fall behind.

In addition to the fine antiques, porcelain, lacquer ware, bronzes, gold and silver coins, figurines from tombs, iron swords and ancient weights, something that caught my eye was a chart showing the various foreign ships that carried opium and the precise amount of their cargo. We knew that British ships were the chief carriers, but one chart indicated that American ships brought into China, in the years 1816 to 1839, a total of 34,513 boxes of opium. Can this be right? Indeed, in checking my history books, I discovered that Yankee traders did profit. The ironic rumor is that their financial gains were reinvested in development of the transcontinental railroad. And guess who bore the brunt of those labors? Chinese immigrants! I confess I was struck with a sense of sadness to learn that American traders were also involved in opium. I remember feeling that same sense of sadness upon hearing that the Governor-General of Hong Kong (a concession to the British as a result of the Opium War), Sir John Bowring, was the same person who wrote the popular hymn "In the cross of Christ I glory, Towering o'er the wrecks of time."

It has been a long and eventful day. We have seen so much in so short a time, and yet it seems as if we have just barely scratched the surface. I keep having to remind myself that Guangzhou is only the first of ten cities we plan to visit. I am looking forward to experiencing the uniqueness of each place. Our energies are charged. But we are grateful for a good night's rest before heading on to Xi'an tomorrow.

Notes on the Economy

Incredible as it may seem to American, European and Latin American economies, inflation has not been a problem in China. Given a controlled market and money supply, prices have remained relatively constant for thirty years. People are able to save money and deposit their funds in a bank account for a 3½% interest yield. Since inflation is not a factor, this interest rate is extremely attractive, when contrasted to the negative return in the U.S. where 5½% interest is offset by a 13% inflation rate.

Money does not seem to be a major problem in China. It is true that salaries are low, but so are costs. Take housing, for example, The average factory worker may earn 60 yuan per month (about $36 U.S.). Housing costs about 3 to 5 yuan per month, which represents a relatively small proportion of one's income—perhaps 3 to 5% or even less, if one totals the number of gainfully employed workers in a household. Compare these figures with the 20 to 40% of income that is spent on housing in the U.S. in these days of skyrocketing mortgage payments.

Food costs run about 15 yuan per person per month. With two or three persons working in a family—plus incentives for extra income, bonuses, profits from the sale of products grown on private plots, and allowance for moonlighting—savings is quite possible and doubtless considerably higher than the meager 3.5% savings rate currently in the U.S. Remember too there are pension rights and free medical care and free birth-control pills! Another major difference: no property tax or income tax in China!

The problem in China is not money, but the shortage of things to buy, even though funds are available. Such scarcity perhaps gives a greater public impression of simplicity and austerity than is actually warranted. Commodities, such as meat, rice, grain, cotton, TV, bicycles or electric fans, are rationed by coupon allotments. Note that this rationing system also controls mobility. Thus if one is unhappy with living in the country-side and takes off for the city, that person will be without coupons.

I was curious to find out about the salary scale and whether there is great disparity of income. Here are some typical salaries we encountered: Our travel guide earns 66 yuan per month and claims that is quite adequate. A senior professor we met is paid 240 yuan per month, or four times as much as an average industrial worker. Another senior professor in Shanghai receives 340 yuan. A junior instructor at the university earns 100 yuan. A senior physician we met earns 280 yuan. A top engineer at a plant we visited receives 180 yuan. A senior mechanic we talked with at a factory earns 80 yuan; his wife is also employed at the same plant. Their combined income is 135 yuan. At an arts and crafts factory, the average salary is 45 yuan. Our 17- or 18-year-old waitresses at the hotel earn 20 yuan—perhaps a reflection of their age and lack of skills.

At the low end of the wage scale are agricultural workers, who earn perhaps half as much as urban workers. Recall that China is essentially a rural economy with 80% of its population engaged in agricultural pursuits. There has been a growing gap between rural and industrial workers. On November 1, 1979, the government sought to bridge the gap by raising prices of agricultural products for city dwellers and giving more subsidy to rural workers. For the first time in three decades, one hears grumbling about inflation from urbanites. Retail prices of pork, beef, mutton, and eggs increased by 32%. The official reason given for this price hike was to stimulate more agricultural production and to narrow the income disparity between rural and urban dwellers.

Perhaps the Harvard economist John Kenneth Galbraith, long criticized for his advocacy of wage and price control policies, would delight in pointing to China, where such policies seem to work.

Economists who study China are impressed by its overall achievements. In 1949, industrial output was microscopic. Today China is the world's third largest producer of coal, cotton textiles, and radio receivers; the fifth producer of steel; and probably the ninth producer of oil. Certainly China is Asia's leading oil producer, surpassing Indonesia, which is known for its offshore finds. Oil experts claim that China is one of the world's last unexplored regions. This is astounding when it is recalled that Western geologists once claimed there was no oil to be found in China. China's known on-shore reserves possibly equal the North Sea and Alaska's North Slope *combined*. Many American oil firms are currently engaged in offshore explorations in joint ventures with China. One can begin to recognize the tremendous geopolitical significance of China as a major oil producer in these days of OPEC dominance. In the late 1980s Chinese oil should come on stream. Already in 1979, crude petroleum was the major U.S. import from China, to the tune of $96.5 million. Paced by booming exports of U.S. farm products (cotton, grain, etc.), trade between the two nations nearly doubled in 1979 to $2.3 billion, compared to $1.2 billion in 1978.

From an economic standpoint, China is currently engaged in restructuring its productive system. Things are changing rapidly as nuclear missiles, heavy machinery, electron microscopes, and computers are being manufactured. With regard to computers, we met several IBM scientists and computer specialists who had been invited by the Chinese government for consultations. Their general estimate is that China is lagging about ten years behind in computer circuitry and about twenty years behind in manufacturing of computers. They also added that leapfrogging was quite possible.

I am inclined to question the wisdom of a general leapfrogging into the 1980s. That may be too great a technological leap. It is more likely that intermediate, small-scale, or even technology of the 60s is more appropriate. Already there is a cutting back from some of the original technological orders from abroad. Moreover, technology should gear in with China's vast supply of labor, rather than displace workers radically.

China also needs to minimize foreign exchange costs and maximize foreign exchange payments. The former can be done through compensatory trade and through focusing on products with a quick payoff that will show rapid results. The latter policy may be pursued through building up of exports of products and resources, especially oil, coal, and light industry. It would appear that the boom in tourism would have immediate payoff. However, I can well imagine that at this early stage tourism's major value is in public relations and not in foreign exchange. Imagine the huge start-up costs of new hotels, an army of travel service personnel, interpreters, drivers, buses, etc.

It will be interesting to keep an eye on China's economic cooperation with capitalists under the auspices of the China International Trust and Investment Corporation. Its president, Rong Yiren, a Shanghai business leader, has circled the globe in coordinating joint ventures and foreign investments in China. One of its many contracts has been signed with the Eaton-Shen Pacific Corporation in San Francisco. Eaton is the son of Cyrus Eaton. This agreement provides for an annual investment of $50 million U.S. for three years on joint venture projects in China.

One other interesting economic note is that competition and incentives are very much a part of new economic policies and practices. Contests of all sorts are staged between production units at the local, provincial and national levels. Workers are paid according to a point system they accumulate. Communes, after fulfilling their quota of sales to the state, may sell their surplus goods at higher prices to the state or at the "free" markets. For example, the state pays farmers a 50% increase for grain sold above the production quota. Wage incentives and competition are being used to spur production. These "neocapitalistic" ideas are innovations which have been stepped up in China's changing economy.

One final comment on incentives in the form of a vignette: At the hotel lobby in Guangzhou, I met an industrial worker who was proudly carrying a framed certificate of achievement. He smiled at me and I asked him what the award meant. He rather modestly responded that he received the award because of his job achievement of producing the largest number of tools in the factory where he worked. Winning this award entitled the worker to a vacation with free stay at the hotel. This sort of recognition is another indication of a rewards and incentive system to acknowledge individual achievement. Apparently the popular slogan "Serve the People," currently being stressed in China, is not necessarily in conflict with rewards for individual effort and achievement.

II

In Xi'an (Sian)

November 14–16

Currently the capital of Shaanxi province, the ancient city of Xi'an is one of the important cradles of Chinese civilization. Founded before the 11th century B.C., at one time Xi'an was the world's largest city. It has served as the capital of China for eleven dynasties. The city is steeped in historic significance. Its present buildings date generally from the 14th century, and its current population is 2.5 million.

After an overview of Xi'an's major towers and temples, we drove out to the newly excavated site of the Imperial Tomb of Emperor Qin (Chin) Shi Huang (221–207 B.C.). In fact, the site of the archaeological dig opened for public viewing on October 1, 1979. How lucky we were!

From a raised platform we had an overview of the digs where some six thousand life-size terra cotta soldiers and horses were discovered. Overhead, a huge structure has been erected to form an exhibition hall covering four acres. The well-preserved pottery figures were buried in an underground vault about a mile from the main tomb, which is still untouched.

More praise for peasants, for the entire find was discovered in March, 1974, by peasants of the local Yan Zhai People's Commune as they were digging a well and struck terra cotta. Pit #1 at the exhibition hall contains over five hundred figures of warriors and five chariots, each one being pulled by four horses. Arms and weapons, such as spears, swords, crossbows and arrowheads, were discovered there. Pit #2 contains an entire pottery-figure army unit of cavalrymen, war chariots and infantrymen. A third pit appears to be the headquarters for the battle formations, which had been neatly arrayed.

This discovery at Xi'an gives valuable clues to the culture, fine arts, military science, and technology of the Qin Dynasty. Despite twenty-two hundred years of burial, the bronze weapons remain sharp and shiny with metallic luster. If what we saw in the outer rim portion of the tomb is so impressive, imagine the dazzling relics that must be contained in the main tomb where the emperor himself resides in regal splendor. Amazing how these emperors sought to immortalize themselves by creating magnificent monuments which are indestructible. In a sense they have become immortal. I would be willing to wager that what will be uncovered in Qin Shi Huang's tomb will be so spectacular that it will dwarf the tiny King Tut remains in significance. Alas, it will take ten to twenty years to complete the project. While we were viewing the first digs in mid-November, it was already too cold for work to be accomplished. Imagine the profound mysteries and fascinating insights to be unearthed. Enough to make an archaeology buff see visions of dancing sugar plums!

"Xi'an Incident"

From ancient archaeological finds, we move next to the Huaqing Hot Springs, which had been a 10th-century Taoist monastery. Set on the side of a picturesque hill, Huaqing has a park-like setting with a central lake, beautiful gardens, delightful paths, and refreshing mineral waters for rejuvenating fatigued bodies and souls. However, its fame today does not reside in its serene and relaxing atmosphere.

It is the site of the well-known "Xi'an Incident," where Generalissimo Chiang Kai-shek, leader of the Nationalist government and the Kuomintang Party, was kidnapped on December 12, 1936, and held captive for two weeks. His life was jeopardized; meanwhile, back at Nanjing, the capital held its breath in the midst of a dual war against the Communists and the Japanese.

Chiang and his entourage were resting and relaxing at this beautiful hot springs, when suddenly one night he heard gunshots. Still in his pajamas and leaving his false teeth behind, he clambered out of bed, went through the back window, and hightailed it up the hills to a hiding place. He was finally discovered and captured in a rocky grotto, which one can detect from ground level only with the aid of high-powered binoculars.

We saw the room, indeed, the bed, where Chiang slept and the window through which he fled. However, we did not have the energy (or the nerves) to climb up to the rocky grotto.

To return to our account of modern history, it was Chiang's own military commnders—a dashing young Marshal Chang Hsueh-liang and General Yang Hu-cheng of the Northern Armies—who did the kidnapping. And it was Zhou Enlai who raced to Xi'an to intervene on the Generalissimo's behalf and negotiated his release—on the condition that Chiang agree to fight against the common Japanese enemy instead of leveling his guns in pursuit of the Communists. In view of Chiang's repeated campaigns against the Communists, the Japanese army had been advancing steadily through China encountering little or no resistance from the Nationalists. Thus the Xi'an Incident was a turning point in modern Chinese history in precipitating a cessation of the civil war in favor of a united front to resist the Japanese.

Despite all the rhetoric on both sides of the political spectrum, I can't help feeling that Chiang and Zhou had a deep mutual respect for one another. Their agreement at Xi'an was an oral commitment.

In any case, the Xi'an Incident is a vivid reminder that from ancient to modern times this capital city has played a crucial role in political intrigues. And with present-day excavations unfolding, Xi'an has a great and glorious past to look forward to. Our family has agreed that Xi'an is a city we will want to return to for a more extended stay.

The people of Xi'an deserve some sort of congeniality award. Everywhere we moved, the people were so friendly and hospitable and open. They gathered around us, smiled, waved and clapped their hands. Little children followed us for blocks, repeating English words and phrases. At the restaurant in the city, we were served a delicious, banquet-style, ten-course meal. Afterwards, the chef and the entire staff gathered to bid us farewell and shake our hands. Our local tour guides went out of their way to be helpful and gave unstintingly of their time and energies. We felt Xi'an's friendliness was genuine. Nowhere else in the world have we met such hospitable people.

It may come as a surprise for some to learn that China is a multi-cultural, multi-ethnic nation. Although the bulk of the population (94%) is derived from the so-called "Han" people, there are some 56 minority groups, including Mongol, Kazakh, Uighur, Miao and Tibetans. At my request, we visited a minority group known as the "Hui" people. If one looks closely, one notes that their skin is whiter than the Han's, and their nose is sharper. Some of the Hui look like albinos.

Interestingly enough, the Hui people are Muslim. About sixty thousand Hui live in Xi'an and about thirty thousand of them center their religious life around the Great Mosque or "Qing Zhen Shi," founded in 742 and rebuilt in the 14th century. Its original stone marker is still intact. Every Friday evening, over a thousand people gather for religious services. Although the leader was away, we talked to some of the believers who were at prayer. The leader's daughter took my daughter Wendy by the hand and raced her into her room on the other side of the grounds in order to give Wendy a present and to exchange addresses. Like others in Xi'an, the Hui people were very friendly.

At the Big Wild Goose Pagoda in Xi'an, site of an ancient Buddhist temple from the 7th century and now filled with room after room of ancient relics, we encountered our own "Xi'an Incident." A middle-aged

Chinese woman was photographing her three teenage daughters when a group of three or four soldiers from the People's Liberation Army passed by and inadvertently blocked the path of her picture-taking. The woman loudly chastised the soldiers and singled out one of them in particular, saying: "Just because you are an officer, don't think you're such a big shot. You're supposed to be serving the people. You're a disgrace to your uniform."* She repeated this, much to the embarrassment of the soldiers. The officer finally replied, "I got out of your way, what more do you want me to do?"

The woman, speaking quite loudly now, continued to scold the officer, even after his comrades led him away from the scene. Then the woman turned to the crowd and, looking straight at me, repeated, "Who does he think he is; his job is to serve the people."

What a scene! I was impressed that the woman had the courage to stand her ground against authority and speak up for her rights; also, the officer was quite apologetic and did nothing to assert authority or arrogance. This indicates to me that despite our mockery of slogans, there is some efficacy to the "Serve the People" slogan, which is found everywhere in public billboards, walls and posters.

Speaking of slogans, the Big Wild Goose Pagoda has another sign of the times. At the main entrance to this park-like pagoda, beyond the front gate and clearly visible to visitors were two empty whitewashed sections of the wall on both sides of the entranceway. These spots were conspicuous by their white color, when the rest of the wall was stone gray. Both of these large spaces once carried strident sayings of Chairman Mao which have now been painted over.

Inside the museum, which featured artifacts from antiquity, several other spots, formerly Mao slogans, have also been painted over. When I rather playfully asked the guide about these changes, his only reply was that those slogans are no longer necessary. Does this not imply that Mao himself has become obsolete?

One other unforgettable incident at the Big Wild Goose Pagoda: As we moved from display to display, viewing a treasure trove of relics from Xi'an's temples and mausoleums, we suddenly came upon two empty showcases. I asked the guide if the missing contents were on loan to another museum. His response created a mixture of embarrassment and fury in my mind. Apparently an American had stolen two ancient and priceless bas-relief carvings, which once guarded the tomb of a Han Dynasty emperor and are now on display at the University of Pennsylvania Museum. If, indeed, they were stolen, as charged, then they should be returned immediately to their rightful owners. Shame on the University of Pennsylvania!

---

*Note that military uniforms in China bear no insignia of rank, as such distinctions were abolished in 1965. Nevertheless, the woman was able to distinguish the officer from the other soldiers.

Visit to Panpo Village

I am beginning to think that Xi'an is an archaeologist's paradise, a seed-bed of vast riches, barely touched. My own excitement in the early human experience is aroused as we visit Panpo Village. This neolithic village dates back to a period of civilization six to seven thousand years earlier. First excavated in 1954, the remains of Panpo are housed in a large, well-maintained (but cold) building with walkways, ramps, and platforms for viewing the so-called Yangshao culture, which is located on the outskirts of Xi'an and overlooks the Chan River.

The remains of Panpo clearly reveal the living patterns of a small village with forty-five homes, cooking utensils, burial grounds for adults and children, stone-age pottery, six pottery kilns, weapons, agricultural implements, stone axes, hunting tools, bone needles, two hundred storage pits, etc. A large quantity of carbonized millet and sorghum grain was unearthed. Signs of a matriarchal clan community are evident in this ancient culture.

Standing at Panpo and taking a glimpse at this way of life, I experienced a strange and eerie sensation. At first, it was the shock of recognition of the affinity between myself and these Panpo dwellers. Then came the sense of joyous affirmation of the link, a feeling of connectiveness that reaches back seven thousand years. We talk glibly and abstractly about historical continuity, but for the first time I could feel it. It was a feeling of identity, of spiritual self-affirmation, of being at one with this ancient people. In a way, when all is said and done, when all the veneer is stripped away, all the masks and pretensions are cast aside, we are not so far removed from primitive existence.

These archaeological discoveries at Panpo remind me of still earlier fossil finds known as "Yuanmow Man," "Lantien Man," and the better known "Peking Man" (*Sinanthropus pekinensis*). As recently as 1967, additional skull fragments of Peking Man, along with stone implements, were unearthed at Choukoutien, southwest of Beijing. My mind still spins with fascination when I realize that these fossils of the earliest primitive existence in China date back four to five hundred thousand years ago.

Parenthetically, I find it rather amusing that the ancient bones of Peking Man are reported to be missing. Imagine that most celebrated archaeological relic is now among the missing persons file! Found originally on a limestone hill just thirty miles from Beijing, the bones were entrusted to the U.S. Marines for safekeeping and for evacuation from China in 1941. At the time there was justifiable fear that the Japanese invaders would overrun China and perhaps destroy Peking as well as Peking Man. Do you suppose that some crusty old marine sergeant has the old bones stored away in his attic along with other World War II souvenirs? Or has the CIA mysteriously entered into the plot, holding Peking Man hostage for some future day of ransom? In any case, the world-wide hunt continues for the missing bones of the old man!

Our experiences of Xi'an make leavetaking from this great city difficult. Our family is filled with awe and utterly fascinated with the early
achievements of the human spirit, which Xi'an in particular and China
in general embody. However, China's rich heritage should not divert our
attention away from the pressing problems and present-day transitional
turbulence and aspirations of its modernization movement.

Notes on Impact of the Cultural Revolution

Everywhere one hears criticisms of the "Gang of Four." They seem to be
the favorite targets for attack. All the evils and shortfalls of the recent
past are pinned on the Gang of Four and the Cultural Revolution they
spearheaded. I can't help wondering whether they are being made con-
venient scapegoats.

The people seem to understand and take the critiques of the Gang in
good stride and even with a dash of humor. After all is said and done,
humor may be China's saving grace. One story making the rounds is
about an ambassador from a European country. This honored guest was
sitting on the speaker's dais. While he was being introduced, the wooden
chair on which he was sitting suddenly collapsed. Stone silence hovered
over the audience. As the ambassador mounted the podium, he looked
over at the busted chair, and muttered, "Gang of Four." Of course, the
entire audience burst out in uncontrollable laughter.

At its best, the Cultural Revolution called for a born-again Chinese
people, recreated in the image of the Yenan spirit, and dedicated to the
Maoist vision of a revolutionary society. It does seem true, however, that
the policies and practices pursued by the Gang of Four had brought
China to a serious impasse, if not to the brink of collapse. Here are some
of the consequences, which are still profoundly impacting the present
situation:

1. Emergence of a "lost generation." I hear many references to the fact
that an entire generation is confused and meandering aimlessly due to
their participation in the Cultural Revolution. At one time heralded as
loyal patriots, this "lost generation" (between the ages of 26 and 36) is
now restless, disenchanted, embarrassed, and without hope. Since the
Cultural Revolution repudiated learning, mocked the professors, burned
books and destroyed laboratories, those who were students during the
heyday of the Cultural Revolution (between 1966 and 1976, with 1966–
1971 the high point) find themselves today without training, skills or
expertise, which are highly valued nowadays in China.

2. We are now seeing the negative fallout and social dislocations resulting from the Cultural Revolution in the form of crime, delinquency,
and protest, especially in the big cities. Many young adult participants in
the Cultural Revolution claim that they gave the best years of their lives
for nothing. They are returning from the countryside in a rebellious,
cynical and disappointed mood. It is estimated that some ten to twenty
million young adults are unemployed. Imagine the letdown felt by many

young people. They have withdrawn into a passive posture in contrast to the heady years of active political involvement. Once they were participants in the revolutionary process, dutifully following the call of their Great Leader. Now they have been reduced to the status of spectators.

3. Another unintended consequence of the Cultural Revolution and the new change of direction under Deng Xiaoping is what might be called "middle management immobility." In a social system where so much of life is regulated, organized, and managed, there is obvious need for a vast layer of government bureaucracy. Wary of fits and starts and sudden lurches in policy, and knowing that Deng is already seventy-five years old, middle management, with an eye to survival, is playing a waiting game. It seems that the modernization drive masterminded by Deng has the enthusiastic support of the older people and the younger generation, but the in-between, middle-aged, middle managers are standing still. They are reluctant to assume initiative or bear responsibility, for they do not want to take the heat if anything should go wrong. This middle management inertia, a sort of failure of nerve, poses a very serious leadership problem for China. The best antidote is a period of stable political leadership—perhaps ten years—for the restoration of confidence. Perhaps a new sense of confidence will enable middle managers to adopt Deng's pragmatic spirit as exemplified in his well-known saying, "It doesn't matter whether a cat is black or white so long as it catches mice."

4. Those who have benefited the most from repudiation of the Cultural Revolution are probably the intellectuals—teachers, scientists, experts, artists and authors. Of course, they had suffered severely when learning was repudiated, education was seen as unnecessary, and art and drama were pure propaganda. Now many intellectuals have been restored to their former positions, professors are valued, learning is given renewed importance, and expertise is deemed essential.

On September 15, 1979, the Central Committee of the Communist Party in China issued twenty-six guidelines or what is referred to as "slogans." Apparently the term "slogan" does not carry the negative connotations that it does in our country. Number 5 reads: "Salute to the workers, peasants, intellectuals, commanders and fighters of the Liberation Army and patriotic personages throughout the country!" For intellectuals to be mentioned at all is a signal victory and would have been undreamed of during the earlier period, save in disparaging terms. To be mentioned right after workers and peasants is indeed an honor!

Slogan #10 is even more explicit: "Take active steps to develop science, education, culture, and health work and strive to raise the scientific and cultural level of the whole nation!" Here intellectuals are given new recognition and status. Repudiation of the Cultural Revolution has meant an intensification of intellectual endeavors, scientific inquiry, and regard for the facts. Indeed Slogan #11 urges: "Emancipate the mind, start up the mental faculties, seek truth from facts, unite and be forward-looking."

It is encouraging to note that Vice Premier Fang Yi held a reception

on September 8, 1979, to honor twenty scientists who have returned
from abroad to work in China. Fang is president of the Chinese Academy
of Sciences and a member of the Political Bureau of the Central Committee of the Communist Party. At the gala dinner meeting, Fang reassured
the returnees that "persecution of intellectuals will never again be tol-
erated."

November 17. Notes on Grief-stricken Relatives

Since leaving Guangzhou, I have been struck by the sense of pathos and
grief on the part of some older overseas Chinese who have returned to
visit their relatives. After a thirty- or forty-year hiatus, the experience is
emotionally overwhelming. At train stations and airports, I have witnessed these reunions between long-separated sisters or brothers or close
cousins. They are poignant experiences of joy and sorrow. Precious
memories of childhood years are rekindled. News of departed loved ones
is shared. Whoever said the Chinese are not an emotional and sentimental
people is dead wrong!

Of particular poignancy are the visits of those overseas Chinese with
their once rich, upper-class relatives, who had enjoyed privileges of
property, servants, and affluent surroundings. I met one such couple and
sensed their grief and compassion. They had visited with their once
wealthy relatives and were overwhelmed by how little they now have.
Forty years ago, the relatives lived in a large, beautiful home, filled with
teakwood furniture; now they live in a two-room house and are stripped
down to the barest essentials; their furniture is meager and decrepit.
However, they did not seem to complain, saying it is best to serve the
interest of the State. But our overseas travelers were grief-stricken.

Of course, it is hard to compare what is with what had been. One must
also remember that many millions of impoverished peasants have had
their lot in life elevated. Once they were living under conditions of un-
bearable poverty with no relief in sight from hunger and disease. I don't
mean to adopt a cavalier attitude, but I am wondering if China hasn't
given concrete reality to the Biblical notion that "the first shall be last
and the last shall be first." At least if the peasants have not become first,
their needs are being more adequately met than at any time in China's
modern history.

I realize that this response does not relieve the anguish of those grief-
stricken relatives who identify with the riches once possessed by their
loved ones. Finally, I suppose, one's view depends upon one's point of
view. Or, as Karl Marx once stated in a perceptive dictum: "Social per-
ception is a function of social location."

November 17. Landing at Yenan

Today we flew out of Xi'an in a propeller airplane. I can't remember the
last time I flew in one of these relics. Actually we had trouble getting

off the ground. A very attractive stewardess reported to us in a friendly, smiling manner that we would have to deplane due to poor weather conditions. We could all see that the mechanics were furiously working on one of the plane's engines. But the wait was worth it. After a brief flight, we landed at the small airport in Yenan—a city of only fifty thousand inhabitants, but famous as the historic site where Mao and his beleaguered troops ended their grueling Long March.

This prodigious feat of endurance has become an important mythic symbol of the Revolution and of present-day China. For those unfamiliar with this history: Chiang Kai-shek launched his fifth "bandit-suppression" campaign against the Communists in October, 1933. Aided this time by a military consultant from Germany, Chiang's forces blocked off the Communists by a strategy of concentric encirclement. Seven hundred thousand Nationalist troops were pitted against three hundred thousand Reds. Led by Mao and Zhou, the Red Army was forced to seek a new sanctuary in order to avoid annihilation. Breaking through the encirclement, the Reds managed to escape the Nationalist trap. One hundred thousand troops began one of history's most dramatic treks. They marched for 370 days, over six thousand miles, through treacherous terrain, across eleven provinces from Jiangxi (Kiangsi) through the Western Chinese wastelands to Shaanxi. Fighting along much of the route, they were bombed and strafed by Nationalist airplanes. Over half of the troops did not survive the ordeal.

What began as a defeat and a retreat, however, wound up as a memorable triumph. New legendary heroes were created by the Long March, as stories of suffering and sacrifice circulated. At Yenan, the Communist Party and the Red Army not only regrouped, but also gained in prestige and attracted growing numbers of admirers to their camp. The Party closed ranks and developed a new sense of cohesiveness, as Mao Zedong emerged as the undisputed leader. Another consequence of the Long March was to bring the Communists closer in touch with the peasants and thereby give flesh-and-blood reality to Mao's contention that the revolution should be built on the base of a rural, peasant's movement. In short, the Long March and the stay at Yenan served to re-baptize and to regenerate the Communist cause in China.

From December, 1935, until 1947, the Communist forces established their headquarters in the caves of Yenan. We could look up and see these very caves where Mao and Zhou and their exhausted troops took shelter. Even at ground level, where we stood, it was exceedingly cold, as we gazed at the cave dwellings in the mountains. The wind was whipping through my down jacket with fury, and I felt chilled to the bone. With their meager resources and battle fatigue, I could well imagine the hardships that Mao and his forces must have endured. No wonder this experience of survival bears such important symbolic significance for the People's Republic of China.

The "Yenan spirit" is a key to understanding the Maoist vision, for the Yenan experience crystallized the virtues of self-sacrifice, self-reliance, hard work, dedication, initiative, struggle for survival, and revolutionary simplicity. Above all, in this cradle of Mao's revolution, the spirit of comradeship was forged. These virtues were subsequently inculcated among the masses. Indeed, one reason advanced for launching the Cultural Revolution in 1966 was to recapture the "Yenan spirit" among a generation who had grown soft and indulgent.

In Yenan, two Westerners are especially revered. Dr. Norman Bethune, a Canadian medical doctor and the son of an Ontario pastor, came to visit and stayed on to join Mao because his convictions led him to cast his lot with the revolutionary movement. Dr. Bethune coordinated medical services, organized medical equipment and supplies, trained others to render medical aid, and performed countless emergency operations at the front lines. In fact, the legendary doctor died from blood poisoning, contracted through a cut in his finger when he performed a difficult operation without gloves. Mao was especially close to Dr. Bethune, whom he praised for his sacrificial life. The moral was clear: If Bethune, a foreigner, could give so unstintingly of himself to serve the Chinese people, what an inspirational model for others to emulate.

The other Westerner is Anna Louise Strong, author of *The Chinese Conquer China*. In Yenan there is a carefully preserved garden spot where Mao met to converse with this American author. She was one of the early visitors who reported favorably about Mao and the revolutionary movement to the American public. For her efforts, Ms. Strong faced disdain and hostility from many disbelieving readers in her own country.

Other prominent authors who journeyed to Yenan for interviews with Mao included Agnes Smedley and Edgar Snow. Snow's sympathetic account in *Red Star over China* attracted widespread attention. Agnes Smedley was a courageous journalist who lived in Yenan in 1937 and wrote about China in such books as *Battle Hymn of China, China's Red Army Marches, Red Flood over China,* and *China Fights Back.* Bethune, Strong, Snow and Smedley are honored in China today as foreign friends of the Revolution.

Yenan is a bit off the beaten path for visitors. However, my hunch is that in the future more and more foreigners will be coming to this holy ground of the Communist Revolution to share in its historic significance. I would not be surprised to find here some day a Holiday Inn to house the tourists! Many will want to explore the Yenan hillsides whose honeycombed cave dwellings provided refuge, to visit the museum of contemporary revolutionary history, and to walk in the footsteps of the heroes of the Revolution—Mao, Zhou Enlai, Lin Piao, Chu Teh and others. Surely travelers will come here to search out those particular caves where Zhou mapped battle plans and where Mao wrote by candlelight many of his thoughts which were destined to become quotations on the lips of hundreds of millions of followers.

III

In Taiyuan

November 17

Continuing our flight from Yenan, we landed in Taiyuan, a city that has grown rapidly to 2 million in population. Located 250 miles southwest of Beijing, Taiyuan is the capital of Shansi province. In the 13th century, Marco Polo visited the city while en route to Xi'an.

My impression is that Taiyuan is rapidly becoming an industrial city. A large steel mill is located here; it employs 12,500 workers. Other plants produce cement, tractors, chemicals, aluminum, iron, and paper. Our first visit was to a carpet factory, which had begun in 1954 with thirteen workers. Today it has grown to over five hundred workers who produce silk and wool rugs. Actually the factory is divided into three large sections. The first is the weaving shop which houses eighty looms, most of which are constructed out of bamboo. We were impressed with the meticulous handwork. A nine-by-twelve-foot rug takes two months for two persons to complete. A day's work is about six to eight inches of progress. But the one hundred or so patterns being woven are beautiful. This is tedious work, but the outcome is quite striking. The work room seemed quite cold, and we wondered what effect this has on the workers' hands. The second section of the factory was a large cutting and knotting room. We made a quick tour through these premises for two reasons. The coal dust circulating around the room from the burners seemed oppressive to our nostrils; and we all covered up our noses to shield against the excess woolen threads and flakes that had been cut by electric scissors and were flying around the air. We felt this was hazardous to our lungs. Both these threats we mentioned to the factory foreman who was escorting us. However, he replied that the workers have safety masks available but prefer not to wear them. Apart from the foul air, the process of cutting and knotting was fascinating for May, who admires this sort of artistry. We did not visit the third section, which is a huge washing and drying room, as it was too early in the day for the washing and drying process to begin.

Our next stop was at the Shansi Provincial Museum. Formerly a Buddhist temple, the museum's extensive grounds consisted of twenty-one separate quarters, each one with well-arranged exhibits. It is possible to spend endless hours in a place like this. Many of the artifacts were from the Ming dynasty and include priceless porcelain, treasures of jade, gold, embroidery, ancient vases, etc.

Then we were taken to the Double Pagoda. This site has some historical interest in that battles raged here between the Chinese and the Japanese and then later between the Nationalists and the Communists. The signs of battle still abound. In fact, there were small pieces of eaves from the roof of the pagoda, built six hundred years ago, that were scattered around the grounds as a result of gunshots. One of the double pagodas had been reconstructed and protruded proudly into the air, perhaps twelve stories high. Work had not begun on the second one. It is interesting to note that during two skirmishes these grounds were embattled because on both occasions the combatants did not feel that the sanctuary-like fortress would dare be attacked. They were wrong twice.

November 17. Visit to the Taiyuan Barber Shop

Each hotel we stayed at in China has a general shop, post office, currency exchange station, doctor's clinic, and barber shop. Of these facilities, the most memorable is the barber shop. A haircut in China is no ordinary, perfunctory cut-and-run thing. It is an experience of having your head pampered and enjoying it immensely. Barber shops serve both men and women, so the customer is as likely to have a female attendant as a male one.

Members of our tour group were so ecstatic about their visit to the barber shop that I finally succumbed and tried it myself. Now I am a convert to the Chinese barber shop! To understand my diffidence, permit me a digression.

I must confess that I am not a barber-shop fan. In fact, the last time I went for a haircut in public was forty years ago. Now that calls for an explanation, for I am not a Rip Van Winkle type, but keep my hair fairly short. At the age of ten, my two older brothers and I went uptown to a barber shop in Burlingame, California, where I grew up in that upper-class community in those days. When we three entered the shop, the barber took one look at us and sneered, "Get outta here, we don't cut Chinamen's hair!" From that day on, my mother cut our hair. Later on, as a student at the University of California in Berkeley, I commuted home to Burlingame on the bus once every five weeks for a haircut from my mother. Still later, when I graduated from the University and married May, she took over this task. There are probably deep-seated scars from that early, traumatic experience of rejection which have yet to be fathomed! In any case, I hope this excursus explains my natural reluctance to visit barber shops.

The haircut itself at the hotel in Taiyuan is not that unusual, except that I noted the barber used an electric clipper, a hand clipper, and then scissors until he was perfectly satisfied that the job was properly done. Next came the wash. Still seated in the same chair, I felt warm water wetting down my hair, and then ever-increasing amounts of shampoo being applied until a thick, smooth lather was formed. For the next five or ten minutes, the barber dug his fingernails into my scalp.

With a hard, scratching motion, his fingernails went back and forth over my scalp, much as a bamboo rake would stroke a lawn. He seemed adept at working over the pressure points. My head was tingling with sensation. Next, the barber chair was tipped back over the sink for the hot water rinse, which was followed by hot towels to the head and face. After the hair was blow-dried and combed, then came the shave.

What a precarious experience, for one who is accustomed to an electric shaver. A sharp razor shaved literally every bit of exposed skin on my face—the cheeks, forehead, nose, inner and outer ear, everything surrounding the eyes. Needless to say, my eyes were shut tight during this ordeal, half in suspense and half in delight. I half expected to see nicks and cuts here and there. Instead there was only a smoothly shaven, clean face.

Then came a vigorous, rolfing-like massage of the forehead, temples, neck and shoulder muscles and arms. When the barber grabbed my armpits, I let out a blood-curdling primal scream that must have startled everyone in the shop. No matter. Now I really felt loose and relaxed. Just what the doctor ordered after a long day's touring. All this service at the barber shop for the unbelievably paltry price of $2.00!

When I returned to the room, my family and friends looked me over and proclaimed that I looked ten years younger!

One addendum to the barber shop experience is worth recounting. My own massage ended at the armpits. However, my vivacious sister-in-law, Bettie, sitting in the barber chair next to me, got more than she bargained for. Of course, there are language barriers and mixed-up communications, but we thought we were both going to receive the same head, shoulder and arm massage. Instead her barber continued to massage beyond her armpits, down her chest, around the rib cage, down to her thighs, and finally her legs! All through this experience Bettie was reclining in the barber chair and did not utter a peep. Good thing she is accustomed to total body massages! To this day, I wonder why he gave her the full treatment and mine was only partial!

Now that we have visited the barber shop, there is one observation that might be made about the general store. Actually these stores are for the convenience of tourists, for they contain the usual personal needs, plus fruits, souvenirs, jade and stone carvings. However, the item that caught my attention was Coca-Cola. Pepsi-Cola seems to have established a beachhead in Russia and Coca-Cola in China.

Coca-Cola may have made an entry into China, but it is not likely that China will be coca-colonized. We were wondering how widespread a consumer item it would be. Just about the only place it can be purchased is in these general stores which are frequented by foreigners. Moreover, the purchase of Coca-Cola requires foreign currency. It may not be bought with Chinese money, but with American dollars in our case. The same is true of American cigarettes and liquor. Coke is an aid to China's foreign exchange problem. What we saw at the general stores throughout China may lead to a sobering insight for the American business community. That vast potentially one-billion-people China market that prompts visions of dollar signs is more elusive than it appears at this point in time!

November 18. Notes on Recent Political Changes

I met with a group of about twelve Americans who have been in China for two months under the auspices of the US-China Peoples Friendship Association. This organization seeks to strengthen friendship and understanding between the two nations. It sponsors shorter study tours in addition to the work/study team with whom I met.

I was eager to dialogue with this group of American young adults who had been working in various communes and factories in a firsthand encounter with Chinese workers. The group was exhausted and seemed to have its mind set on returning home on this last leg of their trip. They were so filled with the immensity of the experience that they were not yet ready to sort out ideas and impressions in an articulate way. One consensus response, however, was their celebration of the openness, the new sense of freedom, and the fact that democracy is growing rapidly in China. This ethos reminded me of an "Open Door Policy," not imposed externally as in earlier history, but established internally. An example was given that the government's TV program even showed a special on the economic progress that has been made in Taiwan to show the Chinese in the People's Republic how Taiwan has advanced in contrast to how backward they still were. Remember that under Mao, Taiwan's economy was painted in disparaging terms. Now the door has swung wide open.

Has it really? This is a continuing question around which much dialogue revolves. Probably there is no clear-cut answer. Those who are more friendly to China answer in the affirmative; whereas those who are like the reporter I met at the beginning of the trip, and other journalists with nostalgic pre-Liberation memories, veer to the negative side.

There does seem to be an undercurrent of unrest at the political level. After thirty years of rule, the major achievement is the elimination of hunger and abject poverty, widespread vice and disease. While this is no mean achievement—in contrast to say, India—with improvements also comes a rising level of expectations. After three decades, many have come to expect more than a subsistence level of living.

The push to modernization by the senior vice premier Deng Xiaoping is recognition of that thrust. China faces the dilemma that stepped-up modernization must depend on outside scientific and technological help, which in turn is predicated upon a more open society. The more contacts that the common people have with the standard of life in places like Japan, Singapore, Taiwan, Hong Kong, and the Western nations—especially through visits and letters from overseas Chinese relatives—the more intense will be the recognition of economic deprivation. At the moment, no effort is being made to conceal this gap. Indeed the discrepancy is being shown to spur the Chinese on to greater levels of productivity.

Deng is striving for immediate and short-term gains that will yield quick results. After all, he is seventy-five years old. Whether he can endure for five more years, and whether Chairman Hua, as a compromise and less aggressive leader, has sufficient strength, remains to be seen. Deng is trying rapidly to establish the new foundations so that China will cross the point of no return. Without equivocation, I would shout, "Long live Deng Xiaoping!"

Obviously the closed-society, anti-foreign temperament of the Cultural Revolution days has given way to a more open climate. Our family feels this in a very personal way. Wherever we move in the streets, stores, or theaters, the people gather around to stare or to converse with us. They are still not accustomed to seeing people from the outside world. They press around to look at our clothing, our shoes, our hair styles, what we purchase, or what we laugh at. We are a happening—less so in the larger cities, but even there, we draw crowds. Groups of people will follow us for blocks in a friendly fashion. I can't help wondering what is going on inside their minds, as they contrast their own simple, austere life style with our wild profusion of colors and individualized styles.

The soundest thing that could happen to Chinese society is a period of political stability for five or ten years. There are bound to be clashes over policy and direction in this post-Mao and post-Zhou era of transition. Deng has the upper hand at the moment. But his policies have to produce results. And I bet no one knows that better than he.

Notes on Doors without Locks

Contrary to earlier experiences reported by China visitors, locks have reappeared on hotel doors. I suppose the earlier practice was too good to be true and simply could not last. At first it was thought that the locks were needed to protect the foreigners from each other. Although that may be true, it is an oversimplified explanation. The fact is, thievery is a human vice not confined to any sector of humanity.

Keys are now needed not just in the larger cities but also in the smaller towns we visited. Usually an attendant at the desk on each floor would be the keeper of the key. Moreover, whenever we entered a crowded store or market outdoors, our China Travel Service guide would warn us to beware of pickpockets, or to hold on to our purses or wallets. Of course, such thievery as there is represents only a tiny fraction of what takes place in America or Europe. Nevertheless, the necessity of locks and keys is another sign of a changing China.

Notes about Museums

Our family is amazed by the countless museums in China. Each province sponsors a provincial museum, similar to the Shaanxi Provincial Museum we visited in Xi'an. Then each municipality and many smaller cities have their own museums. There seems to be an endless and authentic supply of relics and riches kept in these museums.

It is often alleged that the Nationalist forces took the best art objects with them when they fled to Taiwan, or that the museums around the world, such as the New York Metropolitan and London and Paris museums, display some of the finest Chinese collections. However, we still are able to see such marvelous works of art even in relatively small museums.

These collections, dating back four or five millennia, are inspiring and evoke a sense of appreciation of the splendid achievements by the Chinese people through the ages. All these museums prompted my friend, Dr. Bill Lowe, traveling with another Overseas Chinese tour group that criss-crosses ours, to write a postcard to his son with these words of summation of the trip: "Museums, museums, museums; temples, temples, temples; food, food, food." Since each museum and temple has a store to purchase antiques and other art goods, my youngest daughter, Michele, would like to append one other set of words to Dr. Lowe's summary: "buy, buy, buy."

Notes about Crowds, Crowds, Crowds

My daughter Mellanie returned to our hotel to report that when she went shopping in a department store for some gloves, about a hundred people gathered around her in a milling process just to watch her. She was never frightened, for the crowds are friendly and would stand aside and make room for her whenever she wanted to move away. Wherever we go we draw these throngs of curious people. We must look very different to them. We begin to feel as if we are visiting from another planet. One young man came up to Mellanie and kept asking in disbelief, "Are you really Chinese? You look Chinese, but are you really Chinese?"

This ability to attract a crowd of friendly lookers reminds me of the years of mutual isolation during which contact was so minimal. Just about all foreigners draw this sort of attention. In one large city, a Yugoslavian movie star who appeared for the première of his movie must have drawn a wildly cheering crowd of three thousand people. We dashed into our hotel in order to avoid the crush. I suppose we drew added attention because of the five children accompanying their parents. Young Chinese teenagers would come up to them to strike up conversations and exchange addresses.

Probably with the increase in the number of foreign tourists who frequent China, the crowds of the curious will lessen. Already in cities like Shanghai and Beijing this is the case. However, in the interior regions, the crowds are overwhelming. I remember my sister, Rose, and her husband, Dr. Wayne Ho, reporting on their recent visit to the interior near the Tibetan Autonomous Region. They reported that at one town thousands upon thousands of people gathered just to catch a glimpse of them. They took pictures of the crowd, which extended as far back as the eye could see.

When these crowds gather to look, there is never any fear for personal safety. The people are orderly and polite and sometimes will wave and clap their hands. I can't help thinking that isolation breeds curiosity. It is not simply the case of China's insularity. We too have isolated ourselves from China as Americans. The more we get together, the less strange we will be, and hopefully, the less estrangement there will be.

Notes on Slogans

As one travels through the streets, museums, factories and other public places, one notes blank spaces where slogans once appeared. Frequently these spaces have been painted over and faint traces of the original are discernible. Those slogans that have been removed were from the days of the Cultural Revolution. Some of them are Mao's more militant sayings.

The term "slogan" is viewed negatively in our language, but not for the Chinese. Perhaps the more neutral designation "sayings" or "aphorisms" or "teachings" would serve better. I sense that the slogans used on billboards we see all over are used as a teaching tool to instruct the people or to remind them of national goals.

Billboards are nothing new to Americans. By and large, China does not use its billboards to advertise consumer products as we do in such blatant fashion. However, even this is starting to change, and occasionally some commercial advertising can now be seen.

Older slogans, which have now been replaced, exhorted the people to destroy the old traditions or warned them of the enemy imperialists. A typical old-style slogan would read, "Down with American Imperialism and Its Running Dogs." Later on, in Forbidden City, we saw a huge sign, now painted over but still faintly legible, reading: "Don't forget the class struggle. Always remember the bloody past." Another blotted-out slogan said: "Dedicate Your Whole Life to the Revolution!"

Slogans are still being used, but their tone has changed. Now they are aimed at exhorting the people to unite and support the modernization movement, to work hard. Perhaps the most common slogans nowadays are "Serve the People" and "Focus Your Energy on Modernization." Also: "Unite and Build a Modern Socialist Country" and "Peoples of the Third World—Unite." Slogans that relate to foreign countries are now stated in positive terms, such as "Friendship and Unity!" or "Long Live the Great Unity of the Peoples of the World," or "We Have Friends All Over the World." The fact that many slogans mention worldwide friendship and identity with the Third World leads me to suspect that China is making a bid for championing the Third World cause and being its spokesman. Many developing nations have looked to China as a possible model, given its agrarian base and its simple life style. China frequently speaks of itself as a Third World nation, but such nations as Cuba, India, and Angola, which enjoy closer ties to the Soviet Union, would doubtless reject China's aspirations for Third World leadership.

These changing slogans during the past one or two years reflect a new mood in China. It is no longer the belligerent, militant new kid on the block, ready and willing to take on all comers to prove he is not yellow. This is not the strident, bellicose China that offended American presidents from Eisenhower through Johnson, who deemed somewhat arrogantly that a nation that comprised one-quarter of the human race was unfit for membership in the United Nations. The kid has grown up to adulthood and commands his full measure of equal treatment. With maturity comes an appropriate modesty and a desire to set one's own house in order.

Indeed, China's slogans have changed. After all, no one likes to be uninvited to the party, watching on the outside for years with nose pressed against the window pane.

November 19. Meeting with English Teachers from Overseas

At breakfast in Taiyuan, we met an Australian couple who were both teaching English at a local university. Our interest was aroused, for our daughter Mellanie is becoming interested in doing the same thing next year. She would like to teach in Xi'an.

The young couple were primary school teachers in Australia and are currently on leave for a two-year stint. They have been teaching in Taiyuan for eleven months and are living at the hotel where we stay since their promised campus living quarters are just now under construction.

We learned that about four hundred foreigners are involved in similar programs teaching English in China. Of course, these folks have an Australian accent. What they enjoyed most are the students and their high level of interest and motivation. They found the students to be avid learners and fun to teach. Their only problem is the limited teaching resources and materials for instruction. Only one record is available and there are not enough textbooks to go around.

These two teachers are enjoying the experience immensely. Their funds seem very adequate, as each is paid a handsome salary of 460 yuan. They receive free housing but must pay for food. We found this to be a very generous arrangement, especially when compared to salaries paid to Chinese. Each person receives more than a top scientist or high government official. The couple are able to save a considerable sum which they spend on travel to other parts of China. These teachers were scheduled for an additional 100 yuan to match the 15% increase in food costs.

Obviously China wants to treat its foreign teachers well. An example, which may be on the extreme side, is Janet Swislow, who taught English at Wuhan Teachers' College in central China. As a single person, she was given a four-room apartment, two cooks, and a housekeeper. She felt embarrassed by all the privileges lavished upon her.

Later in our journey we were to meet other English instructors from the U.S. They generally expressed mixed feelings about the special treatment, housing accommodations and privileges they received as items that established distance between them and their students. They spoke in glowing terms about the motivation and interest level of the students. One teacher claimed her experience in China is by far the most exciting and meaningful episode in her life. A common complaint was the lack of reading materials for students, most notably contemporary American and British literature. Teachers must innovate and improvise their own teaching materials.

IV

In Shijiazhuang
(Shihchiachuang)

November 19

Shijiazhuang is en route between Taiyuan and Beijing by train. Located in Hopei province, it is less frequented by tourists than any of the other cities on our schedule. After tripping my tongue in trying to pronounce the city so many times, I am convinced that this problem constitutes one reason why it is less popular with visitors! We only stay here overnight.

The countryside leading into Shijiazhuang is scenic and picturesque and filled with cotton fields and apple and pear orchards. Camels are widely used here for pulling carts, and our bus driver gives them a wide berth in passing by them.

Our first visit, prior to dinner, is at the tomb of Dr. Norman Bethune, the famous Canadian medical doctor whom we met earlier in discussions about Yenan. Dr. Bethune's mausoleum is set in a park-like place where many visitors, both foreigners and Chinese, come to pay their respects. In seeing his tomb, we realize how revered he has become in China as a symbol of foreign support for the revolutionary cause. Stories about his heroism and self-sacrifice in caring for the sick and wounded are now part of the revolutionary lore. The Chinese regard Dr. Bethune as a symbol of total dedication to serving the people. Truly he was a man for others.

The only other thing we had time for in Shijiazhuang was an extended visit to a people's commune. In China, there are over 52,000 people's communes, collectively owned and featuring the simultaneous development of farming, animal husbandry, forestation, fishing, and other auxiliary enterprises. Ms. Liu, a woman leader of the commune, and several of her associates greeted us and ushered us into the customary briefing room. One difference this time: in addition to the hot tea and cigarettes, we were invited to taste the apples placed in front of us on the tables. This commune grows several kinds of apples—red, green, Golden Delicious, etc. They were delicious!

Ms. Liu's presentation was by no means perfunctory. We were impressed by her grasp of detailed statistics of output, comparing various years of production, her overall outline of objectives, her general competence, and her poise in response to a flurry of questions. In fact, this is one of many workplaces we visited in China where women play prominent leadership roles.

This commune is so spread out that we had to board the bus four times to drive to its different sections. One section produces honey, nuts, and fruits. Another section was the chicken farm. Still another was the pig sty, which in turn was divided into two parts. The first was the older portion, whereas the second was a brand-new facility that used the most modern methods in raising pigs. Next we went to a mink farm, which evoked our sympathies for the furry creatures—especially since one of the ladies in another Overseas Chinese tour group had rather indecently worn her mink coat for the occasion! In addition, there was a rabbit farm and a large area for raising crops of vegetation, millet, etc.

Communes in China range in size from two hundred to twenty thousand people. This one had two thousand. Its governance consists of three levels of decision-making: the commune, production brigade, and production team. The commune was responsible for overall facilities, such as the primary and secondary school and the hospital. The production team is the basic accounting unit, responsible for its own profits and losses, and decides on production plans and distribution.

Like other agricultural programs throughout China, this commune follows the principles "From each according to his ability, to each according to his work" and "More pay for more work." This is a decided shift from the earlier accent on "To each according to his need." This shift recognizes rewards for individual work. Farmers now have wage incentives and are paid according to their level of productivity. In addition to working on the collective farm, commune members are entitled to cultivate their own small private plots and sell these "sideline" products in the "free" market. In the Beijing area alone, there are thirteen "free" markets where farmers can sell their privately grown produce and pocket the profits.

Hence an incentive system has been built into the production process. Apparently these new arrangements have paid off. In 1979, China recorded the highest food production in its entire history. A bumper grain harvest of 315 million tons exceeded by 11 million tons the old record set in the previous year.

Before leaving the commune at Shijiazhuang, it is well to lift up two items which we saw here as well as at other farming areas throughout China. The first is an ingenious system we encountered, especially in North China where the climate turns very cold, that enables farming to continue during the winter season. In the fields are row after row of hundreds of small plots, perhaps five feet wide by ten feet long and ten or twelve inches in depth. These plots are shaped like rectangular boxes in the ground. The sides are made of adobe. During the winter months, vegetables are grown inside these boxes. Each plot is covered by glass or a plastic material to form small greenhouses to enable the growth of vegetation. Upon seeing this system, members of our tour group kept repeating the old cliché, "Clever, these Chinese."

Another, rather unusual and notable practice, perhaps regarded contemptuously by us profligate Americans, is the recycling of human excrement for agricultural purposes. What is waste to us is valuable to the Chinese! Even the sewage from urban areas is saved in holding tanks and eventually taken to rural areas, ponded, allowed to digest anaerobically, and then used as nutrient-rich fertilizer. We are not referring to the old "night soil" practice. China has begun a simple treating process by piling wastes into tanks to decay until all their toxic bacteria become harmless, while the energy-rich gases are trapped and the remaining solid matter turns to safe, valuable fertilizer. The refuse is capped in specially built tanks called "digesters." While the waste matter ferments to fertilizer, it releases methane gas to be stored and burned as fuel for light and heat. Imagine recycling human waste for both fuel and fertilizer! It may not put OPEC out of business, but it's one alternative energy source that I've not heard or read much about in this country. Perhaps, in a metaphysical sense, Americans do not like to face up to their waste!

If there is such a thing as a model farm, perhaps this commune would qualify. It has a good blend of modern equipment and traditional tools. Its workers seem dedicated to maximizing production. Its animals seem well-tended and healthy. Its average worker earns 38 yuan per month, plus free fruits and vegetables, medical care, pension, and schooling. As we leave the farm, we wave goodbye to our hosts and watch a magnificent setting sun cast its glow over the landscape.

V

In Beijing (Peking)

November 20

China's capital and political nerve center, Beijing is a majestic city of monumental beauty, with a population of 7.5 million. Unlike other cities we have visited, whose temples and museums show signs of deferred maintenance and outright deterioration, Beijing's public places are well-appointed.

Since our quarters at the Overseas Chinese Hotel were still being occupied, we made an "emergency" stop at the Beijing Hotel to utilize their facilities. Wow—what an elegant hotel, equal to the posh places in London, New York, or San Francisco. Its grand style looks strangely out of place in this nation of proletarian austerity. Even though it took all the discipline I could muster, I resisted the temptation to order a strawberry sundae at the Western-style lounge. Thus far on the trip, the food has been almost uniformly good to excellent. I was proud of having lost ten pounds, feasting on many fish and chicken dishes, and wasn't about to surrender yet!

It was seven hours later when our rooms were ready. Beijing is so filled with tourists and visitors that the hotels are jammed to capacity and guides who command a knowledge of the English language are in short supply.

Meanwhile, our bus drove us around to visit the usual sites: Tian'anmen Square, the Temple of Heaven, and, by request, Democracy Wall. Tian'anmen (which means Gate of Heavenly Peace) is a monstrous public square occupying an area of nearly a hundred acres. It would make Times Square look like a sandbox in size. At one end are grandstands, which enable political leaders to review parades, preside over rallies, or view spectacular fireworks displays. Over a million people gathered at this square when Chairman Mao died. Flanking Tian'anmen are many impressive buildings. The Great Hall of the People, where the National People's Congress convenes, is on the western side. To the east is the Revolutionary Museum, which depicts the history of the Communist movement in China, and the Historical Museum. To the south is the Monument to the People's Heroes. Nearby is the Chairman Mao Zedong Memorial Hall, where the body of Mao is preserved in a crystal coffin for viewing by thousands of silent visitors each day. At the northern quadrant lies the famed Forbidden City, where the Ming dynasty emperors, from 1407 onward, and then the Qing emperors, built their palaces of regal splendor. Their secluded palaces contain treasures and riches fit for the "Son of Heaven." Its 250 acres are stunning in architectural beauty and exhibits of fine porcelain, jade, bronzes, paintings, and exquisite art objects that proclaim fine achievements of the human spirit.

Democracy Wall

Democracy Wall is a fascinating symbol of the new openness under Chairman Hua and Vice Premier Deng. Fully three city blocks long, it is a colorful and crowded area, where thousands gather to read the wall posters. Anyone is free to express grievances and complaints. For the most part, the writers sign their names, but we also saw some anonymous postings.

Most of the statements make specific charges against public officials who failed to perform their job properly or were repressive in doing so. Thus one writer accused a particular official of pressure and bribery, while noting that such behavior contradicts the ideals of Communism. Many of the complaints are addressed to the issue of police brutality, false arrest, or arrest without specified charges. Thus one poster charged improper arrest of a seventeen-year-old youth and improper treatment after detention. These writings usually end up with a request for inquiry or for further investigation, and conclude on the note that such police behavior is inconsistent with the teachings of Chairman Mao.

A large crowd gathered around one lengthy hanging, perhaps twelve feet long and four feet high, written in red ink on what appeared to be a bed sheet. This was an open letter addressed to Hua and Deng. Unfortunately the crowd was too dense for us to get close enough to read the poster.

Small knots of people gathered around to engage in animated dialogue, reminiscent of Hyde Park or Berkeley's Sproul Plaza during the 60s. A few vendors were on hand selling their wares.

Another protest spoke about a public official in a province to the north and accused this official of bribery. People with complaints from outlying provinces or from the countryside often come to Beijing to make use of Democracy Wall in hopes of getting more chances for redress of grievances. We saw one such protest from Manchuria. Still another poster writer complained that a Revolutionary Committee had denied him a legitimate livelihood by taking away all his privileges with no apparent reason. One protester listed ten specific charges against a local official. It is apparent that many of the wall posters were directed against the mismanagement or abuses of bureaucratic officials. However, not all the wall posters were critical. A few expressed praise and extolled the virtues of particular officials or policies.

One very strange incident happened to us along the Wall. As we were making our way back from having "surveyed" the Wall's content, we noticed a man staring at us and following us. I had been taking notes and, of course, our style of dress set us apart from the crowd. This man was well dressed and seemed to be in his late thirties. We suspected him to be a government agent. Quickening our pace and looking for the safety of our travel guide, we beat a hasty retreat to our bus.

The man followed doggedly and came to a halt fifteen feet from our bus. Meanwhile, our protective guide from the government's travel service was nowhere to be found! He had taken my children off to survey another section of the Wall in the opposite direction. What to do? Press the panic button? Someone in our group got the bright idea of photographing the man—as if that were the only weapon at our disposal. Just before flashbulbs were about to pop, the man mysteriously made the sign of the cross on his forehead and chest, cupped his hands in a gesture of prayer, while gazing upward toward the sky.

"Jumping Jehovah," I blurted out, "that man's a Christian." Immediately we descended from the bus to converse with him, our apprehensions having suddenly evaporated. His eyes had a glazed stare. He uttered a string of perpetual phrases, words to the effect: "Salvation is in the name of the Lord," "God is our only hope and source of salvation," "Believe in God and you will be saved." These statements were repeated with that same blank stare and eyes lifted upward. Through an interpreter in our group, I tried several times to penetrate his consciousness. Once he responded to my query, if he is part of a Christian group or knows of any churches in the city, by the curt reply that he has no knowledge. Alas, because of the uncommon look on his face, we concluded that this mysterious man may be mentally imbalanced or a fanatic. The mystery remains and to this day I wonder who he is and why we could not communicate.

November 22. Notes on Dialogue about Freedom

Today I had a lively discussion with a Western correspondent about freedom in China. He told me that in the past two weeks fifteen people had been arrested at Democracy Wall. He is rather cynical about the current regime and critical of its repressive tactics. I asked him if it's anything like Russia's labor camps and he agreed it was not.

I accused him of selectivity in his information sources. He is an advocate of political freedom, individual rights, free speech and freedom of assembly in China. I pointed out that the new climate of openness and rapport with the U.S. is certainly an improvement over the recent past. How gigantic can you expect the strides to be? How long has it taken for the realization of freedom for *all* the people in the U.S.?

He asked how much freedom I have felt during our tour. I replied that the freedom we were granted has been total. We are free to wander at will, to talk to whomever we pleased, to raise any questions we wished, to visit anything we asked, save for military installations. Our request to see Democracy Wall was granted immediately.

I am beginning to feel that people from the West commit the myopic error of viewing everything from their own perspective, of judging by external criteria. Doubtless I am guilty of doing the same thing. This is as unfair as a Parisian judging New York City from the bias of his love for Paris (of which it has been said there can be no greater love). It is as if we were to place a grid in front of our eyes, which is American or Canadian or French culture, and let whatever we perceive be filtered through this grid.

My own feeling is that the bulk of the Chinese populace could care less about political ideology, the nuances of political discourse. What they yearn for is a decent livelihood, an improvement of their lot in life. When one considers that China has been ravaged by warfare during most of the 20th century—up to the time of Liberation—by various European powers humiliating the Chinese in carving out extraterritorial rights, by the Sino-Japanese conflict, and the civil war between the Communists and the Nationalists, the lot of the common people, who bear the brunt of war, has not been easy. They want a little peace and tranquillity, a means to earn their daily food, a place to raise their families, and a few amenities in life.

A little stability should go a long way. If the new spirit of openness can continue in force for ten more years, the prognosis is excellent that some alternative political system will be forged that is beneficial to the commonweal and indigenous to the country. Traditionally the extended family pattern, with all its duties and obligations, has deeper roots in the soil of China than does individual freedom.

November 23. At the Great Wall

Here at last—the Great Wall, one of the seven wonders of the world! I can see why millions have come here over the centuries to build, to gaze, to ponder, to conquer or to die. Perhaps China's most famous landmark, this site is now visited by five thousand people per day. The Great Wall is one of the marvels of the world—one of the few unmistakable signs of earth visible to the astronauts from outer space. Apparently only two human-made items are discernible from outer space—the Great Wall and the Los Angeles smog. A visit to the Great Wall is an experience of ecstasy, whereas a visit to Los Angeles can induce tears of pain.

For those unfamiliar with this massive human feat, the Great Wall was begun around 700 B.C. by feudal princes in the North of China. In 221 B.D., under the Qin dynasty, the separate walls were linked together. For hundreds of years this process continued and extensions were made. By 1400 A.D., the Great Wall was essentially as it appears today. It winds its way up and down steep hills and gentle valleys and high mountain peaks across seven provinces for six thousand kilometers. Bear in mind this is the approximate distance between New York City and San Francisco. Its average height is 6.6 meters, while the average width at the top is 5.5 meters—wide enough for five horses to gallop side by side between the battlements at full speed.

At the gate, built of white marble, in the famous pass at Badaling, the student of ancient languages will be thrilled to read inscriptions in Chinese, Mongol, Sanskrit, Tibetan, Uighur, and Tangut, dating from the 14th century. Alas, if the marble stone could only speak, imagine what fascinating tales of battles, of triumphs and agonies could be communicated across the warring centuries to the present-day savagery that still ticks beneath the human breast.

Today, however, on this beautifully clear day with not a single cloud in the deep, blue sky, as we wend our way up the precipitously steep slopes to the top watchtower-fort, huffing and puffing along the way, our thoughts dwell not on warfare. They linger on the sheer aesthetic beauty of a human achievement that is superimposed upon a rugged, natural, primeval terrain and seems to bring into bold relief both the human and the natural.

Like a serpent of stone, the Great Wall snakes its way through the landscape. Its zigzagging wall, meandering through the mountains, also is said to resemble the body of a massive dragon. The sheer scale of the Great Wall is pleasing to the eye and inspiring to the heart, which is still pounding from the ascent to the top watchtower. From here, it seems as if you can see forever into the limitless horizon.

As we reach the high watchtower, where individuals gather for photographic proof of their presence here, my ears detect many tongues, chattering excitedly, from different nations—Germany, Rumania, Italy, Japan, Albania, France, Portugal, America—a veritable Tower of Babel. One exuberant American, in his mid-sixties, expressed his childlike joy by standing on his head, while his wife obligingly captured his pose on camera. He happens to be a stockbroker–pension fund manager from Baltimore doing his thing at the Great Wall. What a grand sight for his grandchildren!

In many respects, the Great Wall, like the Biblical Tower of Babel, is the human endeavor to achieve immortality. It is awesome and breathtaking. By the grace of God, this human landmark, though badgered and buffeted through the ages, remains standing as a monument to human achievement. Perhaps now I have a clue to the meaning of the old saying about Venice: "To see Venice and to die." To see the Great Wall of China and to live is an ultimate experience.

November 24. Notes on Special Privileges for Foreigners

Our family has been discussing our mixed feelings about the special treatment accorded to foreigners. Although we are the grateful beneficiaries of this practice, it still makes us uncomfortable.

Apparently travelers from abroad are classified into three categories: foreigners, overseas Chinese, and Chinese who reside in Hong Kong, Macao, and Southeast Asia. Although the best hotels and facilities are reserved for the first category, in fairness, there is also a descending scale of fees charged.

Locked gates at the railroad terminal are quickly opened for our bus to deposit us on the platform right next to our train, while crowds of local people wait outside the gate. At the movie theater or opera house or stadium, we are ushered to special reserved seats, which are the best seats in the house, while natives are seated to the rear or in the side aisles' seats. Audiences usually politely permit us to depart first after a performance. At airports and rail stations, we are escorted to the VIP rooms, where hot tea is served. At one performance, after being ushered to special seats, the production was delayed until the arrival of another overseas Chinese group. Then the spotlight was turned on the late-comers! Wherever there is a line of people awaiting their turn, we are taken to the head of the line.

All this preferential treatment does not sit right with us. I suppose this is the Chinese way of honoring a guest with extreme courtesy and hospitality. Doubtless we in the West could learn something from this cultural practice, which is akin to the Biblical dictum of extending hospitality to the stranger at the gates. In our own American spirit of individualism, each person for himself/herself, we tend to overlook special courtesies to visitors and foreigners in our midst.

At the same time, this practice of deferential treatment for foreigners in China evokes unpleasant memories of the days of extraterritoriality, when Westerners enjoyed privileges and behaved with impunity and lived like sheiks.

Hopefully, those days of utter humiliation have been relegated to the dustbin of history. Nevertheless, I can well imagine resentment and hostility building up—especially since only a few short years ago, foreigners, and particularly Americans, were scorned and cast as villains and devils. Now they are granted preferential treatment. An American seemingly can do no wrong in China. The flip-flop from being regarded as enemy to friend is nearly as quick as it takes for a ping-pong ball to sail over the net. I hope this does not mean blind adulation; for what is uncritically accepted can be similarly rejected—if the pendulum should swing back the other way!

A cursory examination of history could turn an optimist into a cynic, when one considers the orchestration of various mood responses by Chinese and Americans towards each other over the past decades. Recall that during the Korean War, the Vietnam War, and the Cultural Revolution, the Chinese regarded Americans as "arrogant villains," "paper tigers," and "capitalist imperialists." Americans in turn have ridiculed the Chinese with such expressions as "yellow peril," "mysterious Fu Manchu," "anthill society," "Communist bandits," etc. For decades, Americans have been nursing a wounded (though false) pride that we "lost"

China, as if it were a possession of ours to lose. Now we are enjoying a honeymoon period. Military leaders of both nations are speaking of co-ordinating their efforts, moving "in concert" and along "parallel" lines. Perhaps it would be unrealistic to expect this climate of euphoria to continue indefinitely. Indeed, perceptive writers in both countries have pointed to the alternating love/hate ambivalence that has characterized relationships between China and the United States over the years.

November 24. At the Beijing Opera

Being at the Beijing Opera is not what the typical Westerner would call the most exciting way to spend an evening, for the acting seems ponderous and the tonal quality strangely unfamiliar to our ears. I can imagine the reaction of a Chinese attending a hard rock concert for the first time!

Actually, Beijing Opera is an ancient art form, a way of transmitting history and customs through the oral tradition to a largely illiterate people in the past. The opera requires amazing skill on the part of the performers, since it combines singing, acting, few props and much imagination, dialogue, and acrobatics. Its stylized techniques are refined, its costumes colorful and elaborate, and its music dramatic.

For quite another reason, this experience of Beijing Opera is significant because it underscores another shift that has taken place in the field of drama and entertainment. Just a few years ago, under the managed art of the Cultural Revolution, classical Chinese opera was a "no-no." This evening's is now the fifth performance we have attended in various cities. In none of these shows was there the slightest trace of propaganda or indoctrination or even opening with the national anthem—a not uncommon procedure for entertainment/sporting events in the U.S.

Earlier reports by Western correspondents noted that Chinese drama and art were flawed by the heavy "message" of furthering ideology, or that the music had a martial quality that was offensive. Perhaps this criticism has gotten through to the Chinese artistic community, for the change has been dramatic! Or, more than likely, the heavy hand of Mao's wife, Jiang Qing, one of the Gang of Four, has been removed from domination over the artistic field. As a result, we now have a depoliticization of the theater.

Beijing Opera's performance this evening featured a classical story best described as a romantic fairy tale. There is a death scene, filled with tragedy at the climax; then the dead heroine returns as a ghost. A young worker in his twenties, sitting nearby in the audience, was overheard to remark that he found this sort of drama exceedingly difficult to understand. Indeed, fairy tales and ghosts would seem absurd to the younger generation. On the other hand, the older generation not only understood, but were familiar with the plot and could identify with this classical story.

Only one change had been made in the entire drama. Instead of being

a poor scholar (I suppose scholars are no longer poor!), as in the original
script, the hero was a poor fisherman.

Tonight's performance is symptomatic of the decided shift in the artistic world since the Gang of Four's demise. Ten years of stifling censorship have given way to a restoration of an openness that brings back
memories of "letting a hundred flowers blossom and a hundred schools
contend" in the fields of art, literature, films and drama. Themes that
were once taboo are now receiving artistic attention.

Even the once ridiculed music of Beethoven is now in tune with the
new openness. In late 1979, Seiji Ozawa conducted the Beijing Central
Philharmonic Orchestra, which performed Beethoven's Ninth Sym-
phony for the first time in nineteen years. Many other foreign artists
from America, Europe, and Japan have been invited to perform.

Another new feature in the entertainment field is foreign films. Charlie
Chaplin classics are a hit. *The Kid* (1921), *The Circus* (1928), *The Great
Dictator* (1940), and *Limelight* (1952) are playing to appreciative audiences. One member of another Overseas Chinese tour group went to a
local movie theater on his own one evening to see a Japanese film. He was
surprised and even shocked by the scenes of explicit lovemaking and
scantily dressed actresses he saw on the screen. It seems as if Chinese
movie-goers have an ever-enlarging choice of American and other foreign films to see these days. In view of the sudden turnabout to more
revealing foreign films with themes featuring love and violence, it would
not be surprising to me for the more puritanically minded Chinese to
pull back from some of the more risqué films that seem to be standard
fare in foreign filmmaking. In any case, the tolerable limits are bound to
be tested in this time of openness.

November 25. Notes on Self-Reliance

Self-reliance is the doctrine of national self-sufficiency, which is one of
Chairman Mao's better-known teachings. It seems to have reached certain limits—especially in the fields of science and technology.

To be sure, Mao's early emphasis on self-reliance has served a useful
purpose in galvanizing the people to action, to change their condition in
life, instead of adhering to a spirit of resignation that accepts abject
fatalism. One of the favorite Chinese sayings in the past is the fatalistic
comment, "That's the way things are; nothing can be done about it."

As a poet and a revolutionary, Mao instilled and inspired a spirit of
self-reliance which conveyed a sense of "can-do" to overcome the negative "can't do" mentality. Self-reliance means that people can take fate
into their own hands and be masters of their own destiny. A proud product of the self-reliance principle is that since 1960, when Soviet aid
terminated, China has achieved its remarkable gains without outside
help.

Yet it seems foolish, having come this far, not to tap the known, tried
and tested ways. Now, I suspect, the common-sense, pragmatic, even-

tempered legacy of Zhou Enlai comes to the fore in the realism of the modernization movement. (Incidentally, we have gone into a numbr of homes of intellectuals in China which have the portrait of Zhou hung proudly on the wall, but not Mao's. Indeed, it is a good thing for chairmen to step down and retire before they become obsolete.)

On the limits of self-reliance, a case in point is the block of apartments constructed only last year in Beijing. It seems that water cannot rise beyond the second floor in this seven-storied building. Moreover, there are so many engineering and structural defects that a German consultant, called upon for advice, recommended that the entire structure should be torn down and done right the next time.

The Maoist maxim of self-reliance notwithstanding, China has discovered in recent years an interdependent world in which no nation can go it alone. I suspect the Chinese officials recognize the shortcomings of total reliance upon self-reliance and are moving quickly toward a greater degree of interdependence in various spheres of life. To call this revisionism is just plain silly.

In Wuxi (Wushih), we met a group of about a dozen burly construction workers who took their meals at the table next to ours in the same hotel for foreigners. They didn't look like your standard foreign tourists. When we got acquainted and swapped stories, we discovered that even though China has a superabundance of laborers, these all-white tradesmen were imported from Australia to build another hotel for tourists! Surely this does not accord with the older understanding of self-reliance. Just as surely, you can bet that the Chinese will be watching to see how these "blokes" (as they referred to themselves) do the job.

Chinese students are being sent abroad in sizable numbers for advanced study, especially in the scientific and technological fields. When they return home, they should have a profound influence and contribute further to the growing spirit of innovation and openness.

November 25. At Forbidden City

Forbidden City was the seat of power for the last two imperial dynasties—the Ming and the Qing, who ruled with absolute authority for more than five hundred years, until Sun Yat Sen's revolution, which inaugurated the modern period in 1911.

At Forbidden City, we encountered undreamed-of grandeur and magnificence—carved marble steps, sculptured animals, golden temples, jade thrones, and buildings clustered with an exquisite sense of proportion and design. Standing here in the midst of priceless riches and the many splendors and impressive palaces of Forbidden City, I could not repress two sudden feelings. An immediate and rather haughty thought occurred to me that when Europeans were still a tribal society, the Chinese were already enjoying a high civilization, dressing in silk, and eating from porcelain bowls. Then, while gazing at the elaborately decorated ceremonial halls, where the emperors held court, how I wished that these walls could speak, for they would whisper sagas of centuries of political intrigue within Forbidden City. In that respect, politics in China or elsewhere has not changed much!

Never before have I viewed such fabulous treasures. Might it be that common people were forbidden from entering these gates because the Ming and Qing emperors really did not want them to know the extent of the riches sequestered within these walls, lest resentment and revolution be fomented?

So much gold gathered in one place! Entire blocks of gold, gold ingots, bowls, vases, headdresses, chopsticks, banners, leaves, sixteen two-foot-high gold bells, etc. I have counted at least thirty huge urns—perhaps five feet high and five feet in diameter—scattered around the palace grounds. At one time these urns were filled with sand and water and used as resources for fighting fires. About 150 ounces of gold were used to plate each urn. Today only the faintest traces of the gold remain. In beating back the Boxer Rebellion's efforts to rid China of foreigners, the victorious Western soldiers scraped off the gold while ransacking the Imperial Palace. The United States was a party to this conquest and subsequent looting, along with England, France, Japan, Russia, and Germany. A protocol imposed upon China and signed in 1901 allowed ten foreign governments to station troops in Beijing. My mind drifted back to the gold-plated urns. Imagine 150 ounces per urn and thirty of them at current prices gyrating between $460 and $880 per ounce!

If the precious, yellow metal is not to your liking, then look at the displays of priceless pieces of jade of every variety, shape and color, and of exquisite quality fit for emperors! Dazzling are two mounds of jade, which stand about five feet high and four feet wide, and are intricately carved into mountain scenery. Nine years of labor were consumed to finish one of these jade mounds. Now that I have seen what is referred to as "imperial jade," everything else suffers by comparison. Its dark green, translucent quality is aptly described as the "Stone of Heaven."

Now if gold and jade are not your cup of tea, then feast your eyes on diamonds, rubies, pearls, ivory, coral, sapphire, and other precious stones. If all this is not sufficient, then look to the fine masterpieces, original paintings, cloisonné, porcelain, antique dishware, bronzes, scrolls, and embroidery.

It occurred to me, somewhat facetiously, that if China faces a foreign exchange problem, here is the solution, contained in its own treasures at Forbidden City! But God forbid!

It is difficult to imagine that all the splendor we have seen here has already been diminished by lootings on the part of various Western powers and by the Japanese. In addition, thousands of crateloads were carted off by Chiang Kai-shek's forces to Taiwan on the eve of Liberation in 1949. Incidentally, some of these goods are on display on a rotating basis at the museum in Taipei, Taiwan.

Now the common people of China and foreign visitors alike have access to Forbidden City. No longer sacred ground, it is open for their viewing of its grandeur and its opulent treasures.

I could not help feeling that a nation whose greatness and glory are evident in the high degree of civilization achieved in the past will once again have a bright future. Some day the phoenix will rise again!

Notes on Museums and Unexcavated Tombs

All the museums, temples, public parks, and tombs of the emperors that we visited everywhere in China were crowded with both native and foreign visitors. The crowds were orderly and one had to look hard to find signs of police around to guard the precious relics.

At the Ming Tombs, for example, one large showcase was filled with solid gold pieces—ornaments, blocks of gold, gold vases and bowls. I, looked at this dazzling display of a mini–Fort Knox store of precious value. Then my eyes cast furtively about for the presence of Pinkerton-type armed guards. Unless they blended with the woodwork, no guards at all were even present. Trusting, these Chinese!

I was informed that what we saw was only a small portion of the gold pieces of one particular emperor. The nearby tombs of twelve other Ming emperors are still unexcavated. Moreover, no present plans are on the drawing boards to move ahead with excavations in view of the paucity of funds. Imagine, twelve other mounds, each one with elaborate entering gateways to the unearthed tombs and visible as one approaches the area. Truly there is gold in them thar hills!

In addition to what is on view at the one excavated Ming tomb, other precious gems and artifacts from this particular tomb we visited are on loan to museums throughout China and across the world.

Two reflections: In a way it's a shame that other excavations are not being planned. If it's a question of funds, I note that admission to these places is either free or only ten fen—equivalent to about seven cents in the U.S. I don't see why foreigners shouldn't be charged 50 cents or even $1.00 for admission. With the many foreigners we saw from all over the world jamming these facilities, in due time a substantial fund would accumulate for additional excavations. I trust this suggestion is not simply a capitalistic ploy, but one that benefits all humanity!

Perhaps this is the time and place to take issue with a one-sided, cheap-shot article by David Finkelstein in the *New Yorker,* September 10, 1979, issue. As an affluent American traveling in China, Finkelstein is always muscling his way to pay the cheapest prices in trains or restaurants, wishing to pay what the natives are charged. He is a Ford Foundation consultant on China (gads!). I don't suppose he would want to trade salaries with the natives. What gripes me is that once this Finkelstein succeeds in getting his way in paying the lower prices for food or transportation, then he proceeds to complain about the inferior quality or poor accommodations. Come on, David. You can't have it both ways. I don't know what this New Yorker is trying to prove. But I personally found his article offensive, arrogant, patronizing, ideologically tainted, and a pseudo-sophisticated version of the "ugly American." All this in a magazine I've always admired!

A second reflection: When I gaze upon such splendor and riches uncovered from the various emperors' tombs, the realization dawns that all
this grandeur did not appear out of thin air. Someone paid a heavy price
—in money or labor. Indeed, the emperors ruled with such absolute
authority that they exacted heavy tribute and taxes from the people.
Small wonder that through the centuries peasants have periodically re-
volted. At times these upheavals were crushed unmercifully; at other
times, they succeeded in toppling a dynasty.

November 26. At the Summer Palace

Beijing is truly the city of palaces. There is even one for the summer-
time, where royalty could come to enjoy the cool breezes and escape
Beijing's oppressive summer heat. Unless one is a dévotée of ice-skating,
the Summer Palace is hard to take in the winter time. The cold air rushes
off the human-made lake and cuts to the bone. The winds are biting and
violent.

All sorts of interesting sights dot the extensive landscape of 660 acres.
Palaces, pavilions, temples, and rock grottoes are plentiful. Along the
lake, we found a fascinating walkway that was covered with over a hundred beams on which were painted historical and mythological events
that traversed the whole history of China. This was an educational experience per se. Were it not so blasted chilly, I would have loved to
linger longer on these scenes. Fortunately the walkway led directly to a
warm restaurant where we feasted on a banquet-style lunch.

Fully refreshed, we were on our way again to the water's edge. Alas,
we came to the famous marble boat, built under the direction of the
Empress Dowager Ci Xi (Tzu Hsi) in 1888. What an act of incredible
audacity for her to divert funds which were earmarked for building a
navy so as to do battle against Japan. Instead the empress created an elegant, luxurious marble ship to satisfy her own selfish needs. Here she
could come to sip tea, while enjoying the cool breezes from the lake.

As it turned out, China lost the war against Japan in 1894 and had to
surrender territorial concessions and rights that were not to be recovered
until after World War II. The Empress Dowager incurred the disdain of
the Chinese people for her self-serving needs. But, ironically, she has
won the admiration of future generations of tourists for having created a
singular work of consummate beauty. One might say that she lost a war
but has carved out for herself a monumental place in history. Look at it
from a visionary perspective. The Empress Dowager had the foolish
audacity to turn swords not into plowshares but into a toy marble boat.
Imagine what the world might be like if *all* military spending by sove-
reign powers were sidetracked into equally ridiculous projects. Perhaps
we would be better off!

*
* *

At the Museum of the Chinese Revolution

Some visitors to this museum might consider it a propaganda center to extol the virtues of the Communist Party. Actually it is quite an interesting place for most of us who know so little about the struggles of the Communist revolution that led to what is known as Liberation. Of course, there is a slant to the story, much as a museum in the southern United States might express its side of the War between the States. To the victor go the tales!

This museum covers quite a large floor space. Yet the space is filled with memorabilia, documents, war relics, simulated battle situations, horror chambers used by the KMT, etc. Indeed, the entire history of the Chinese Communist Party from 1921 to the present day is unfolded here.

I'm not sure why, but the museum was forced to close down during the period of the Cultural Revolution and was only reopened to the public on October 1, 1979. Founders of the Communist movement, such as Li Dazhao, Cai Heshen, and Mao Zedong are prominently featured. Those who have fallen from grace, such as Liu Shaoqi and Lin Biao, are conspicuous by their relative absence.* Mao's exploits are recounted in intimate detail. My impression is that everything Mao ever did or wrote or wore or planned is here. Of course, this is a hyperbolic statement, but the impression is still strong.

The Long March is reconstructed and given dramatic and graphic display. Many of the displays in this museum are military in nature, portraying weapons and paraphernalia used for battle.

Perhaps one reason it took so long for the museum to reopen is the extra time required for revising recent history. The new exhibition succeeds in repudiating Lin Biao and members of the Gang of Four and exposes their fallacies. It shows clearly that the history of the Communist Party in China is one of a struggle between two conflicting political lines.

Apart from the displays, I was impressed with the large crowds here. I have in mind crowds of Chinese spectators. Many army personnel must take their vacation or day off roaming these halls. Busloads of school children come to the museum with their teachers. By and large, the pupils are orderly and busily engaged in taking down notes in front of various displays. A few of the children are on the playful side and prefer to engage in a hide-and-seek-type game. One particularly effervescent teacher must have lectured his students for a half hour in explicating one of the decisive battles being depicted. He was a real spellbinder and seemed to recreate the events in very dramatic fashion. We passed by him, and when we circled back much later, the teacher was still going strong.

---

*Note that under Deng's leadership, Liu Shaoqi has been posthumously restored to a place or prominence.

November 29. Notes on Learning English

The English language was never more popular in China than at present. Everywhere one hears young people practicing their pronunciation. At sales counters, in restaurants, near schools, even in the elevator, and wherever young people gather, they are eager to test out their skills in repeating English words.

They listen to the TV for evening English lessons or to the radio or to cassette tapes with English instructions. Unlike the Japanese, with whom we stayed in Japan for a year, the Chinese seem adept at picking up English and will seize the opportunity to test out their skills. I can see that if one is shy or afraid of making mistakes, learning languages comes harder. The more outgoing Chinese are avid learners.

Our family members have practiced vocabulary with many Chinese in nearly every city. We are impressed by the number of self-taught English-speaking persons we encountered. Our tour guide in Nanjing (Nanking) is a good example. He formerly taught Chinese languages at Nanjing University. For twelve months he instructed himself by listening to the TV and radio, following a grammar book he had bought, and using a Chinese-English dictionary. During the three days he spend with us, he would write down on a card every new word he heard, pronounce that word many times, and then use it in a sentence for us. Actually, he is quite good. However, words like "unusual," or "worry," or "allure" or "wary" were difficult for him and others to master.

The only trouble is that the spirit is willing but the resources are weak. Both books and instructional guides are desperately lacking in quality and quantity. Some of the books are embarrassingly dated. For example, one widely used text repeatedly refers to blacks in the U.S. as "niggers." Many of the Chinese are unfamiliar with the connotations of this derogatory term. We found it offensive and told our guide, who promised to relate this information to the proper authorities.

Another difficulty for Chinese trying to master English is the American idioms or slang expressions they come across. For example, one avid learner approached me for help to understand a word he had read in a recent American magazine. When he looked up the meaning of the word in an English dictionary, he was baffled. He asked, "What is the meaning of the word, 'sucks'?" When I asked for the context or how he saw the word being used, he said he read a banner that said, "Ayatollah Khomeini Sucks!" "What does this mean?" Imagine trying to explain that! Doubtless an entire course could be offered on American slang expressions.

I am impressed with the relatively good job the Chinese are doing in their efforts to master the English language. Think how much more they could do with modern technology, recordings and audio-visual equipment at their disposal. Consider also the dire need to upgrade textbooks. Priority is currently given to teaching and learning English in the educational system. Note that the primary, secondary, and collegiate levels embrace over 210 million students—nearly the size of the entire U.S. population! Think of the staggering potential textbook market for that many students. Chinese educators believe in adopting one standard, uniform text for a particular grade for all the schools. Can you possibly imagine a textbook printing of ten million copies? I'm surprised American publishers aren't tripping all over themselves trying to break into this enormous market! Of course, they will have to learn about joint ventures and devise a way to bring prices for books way down!

November 26. At the Underground City in Beijing

If centuries earlier, construction of the Great Wall was an engineering feat, consider the marvel of building a vast underground city, literally by human hands, in Beijing today. I wonder how many people realize that an entire network of underground tunnels and cavernous spaces exist as a shelter in the event of a nuclear war or other catastrophe that seems to be anticipated.

We feel particularly privileged in making this visit to the underground city, especially since the guide informs us that "only our good friends are shown" this site. Started in 1965, the underground city is still being expanded by volunteer laborers, following a full day's work at their regular jobs. At present there are three levels, which can accommodate 3.5 million people who can be evacuated to the subterranean levels in just five minutes! This is just unbelievable. I'm not sure which is more incredible—the place itself or the prospects of having to use it for a catastrophe.

Concealed entrances to the tunnels are scattered in over nine hundred places around Beijing—in stores, factories, schools, and public buildings' A clerk pressed a button behind a sales counter in a department store and presto—suddenly a section of the floor slid open, and away we went, down a flight of descending stairs underground. These incredible tunnels cross the length of the city of Beijing from east to west and then extend to the caves in the mountains. Boxes of food are stored underground and generators provide electricity and clean air. The whole thing is mind-boggling. Perhaps fifty years from now, when tourists are shown Beijing's underground city, they will marvel, much as today's visitors express awe at the Great Wall. We leave Beijing on an ominous note, wondering if there will ever be a use for its underground city, and dreading the thought.

VI

In Nanjing (Nanking)

November 26

We arrive by train in Nanjing, a city of over two million people, situated on Changjiang (the Yangtze River). Nanjing is the capital of Jiangsu (Kiangsu) province. With a history of over 2,500 years, Nanjing was one of China's ancient capitals and has served that role also in modern times. Sun Yat Sen made Nanjing the capital of his new Republic and so did Chiang Kai-shek during World War II, when the Japanese occupied Beijing.

Nanjing's wide and picturesque streets are marvelously laid out with an abundance of shade trees on the side. Its main street consists of four lanes—the central lane for trucks, buses and cars; the next lane for push carts; followed by a lane for bicycles; and then a lane for pedestrians. Along the side lanes, mule carts and an occasional flock of geese add more color. Moreover, there are traffic circles with central fountains, statues, and flowers blooming.

After visiting some of the usual sights—temples and museums—our children expressed a yen to see the zoo, which we had passed up in previous cities. Their idea was that one cannot go to China without paying a call on the panda bear. We were immediately taken to the Nanjing Zoo and were not disappointed. We caught the giant panda bears as well as smaller pandas in a feisty, playful, frolicking mood. Visiting the zoo was a change of pace for us. My children's only critical comment was concern for the close quarters or confined space in which the animals were kept.

Next we toured the Nanjing Bridge. Now it needs to be said that this is no ordinary suspension bridge. One of China's proudest achievements is the completion of the Nanjing Bridge, which crosses Changjiang and forms an important link between the lower Changjiang region (including Nanjing and Shanghai) and Beijing. Two reasons account for China's pride in this bridge. Western engineers had said it was impossible to build the bridge in view of the water depth and bedrock conditions. Then the Russians abruptly withdrew their technical aid and financial

Above: Guangzhou, Chrysanthemum Gardens. (All flowers from one stock)

Left: Graffiti in bamboo, Tsung Hua Hot Springs.

Left: Free market vendors in Guangzhou.

Below: Lee Family at the Great Wall.

Left: Tile eaves in ancient temple in Taiyuan.

Below: Wall posters at Democracy Wall in Peking.

Left: On the road to
Ming Tomb.

Below: In the For-
bidden City.

禁止攀

Above: An iron turtle
in the Forbidden City.

Left: A gilded lion
in the Forbidden City.

Primary school children in Nanjing performing.

Street-cleaning machine in Shanghai.

Two members of the ancient "Gang of Four" at Yue Fei Temple in Hangzhou.

Terraced Dragon Well Tea Field in Hangzhou.

"Camel Hill" in Guilin.

The author with five pastors of the Drum Tower Union Church in Hangzhou.

support for the project. So the Chinese were left high and dry and had to go it alone.

China accepted this challenge as another "Long March" and accomplished the improbable engineering feat. Hence the beautiful double-decked Nanjing Bridge stands today as a model of the self-reliance principle. It was good for China's morale and confidence. It takes an hour just to walk the length of this newest and largest of China's bridges. On this cold and windy day, we were not about to attempt the hike.

As delightful as I found the bridge, temples, Sun Yat-sen's Memorial Park, the city's numerous gates, and the factories and antique shops that we visited, I was more eager to keep a personal rendezvous.

Notes on Visit with a Friend

In the evening, May and I went to visit Sui Mei Kuo, whose husband, Bishop K. H. Ting, visited on our campus and in our home just last month during his visit to the U.S. and Canada. I had worked with Sui Mei thirty years ago when she served as Executive Director of the Chinese Students Christian Association and I was its Western Regional Director. That was my first paid professional job, if one excludes waiting on tables in the family restaurant.

I was eager to see how Sui Mei had changed from my memories of her as a vivacious, gracious, and captivating woman full of energy and enthusiasm. Our reunion was therefore a very thrilling moment. Slightly thinner, she is still vivacious, attractive, and gracious. Her eyes are full of sparkle and her manner of speech animated. She is quick to initiate or to join in laughter. When I reminded her that she was my first "boss," she replied that she hopes she had been democratic. Unfortunately, Sui Mei has been suffering from rheumatoid arthritis, on top of which she recently fell and fractured her hip.

Naturally we reminisced about old times and mutual friends. Sui Mei has been a professor of English at Nanjing University. Since her immobility, her students have been coming to her home for instruction. Once the residence of a missionary, the Tings lived here while he was president of Nanjing Theological Seminary. During the Cultural Revolution, however, the home was occupied by ten families. Sui Mei suggested that the Cultural Revolution era persisted for thirteen years, from 1965 to 1978, when it was officially repudiated. It has taken a while to regain properties that had been occupied, since persuasion rather than coercion is necessary.

It felt warmly good to be in touch with old friends again, after such a long hiatus. While we were visiting with Sui Mei, K. H. Ting was landing at the Beijing Airport. I hope we can stay in touch with the Tings.

*
**

Notes on Various and Sundry Street Scenes

Nanjing, like other cities in China, is filled with fascinating street scenes. One of the first stunning sights is the thousands of bicycles, moving in unison with their rhythmic bells perpetually ringing. Imagine Beijing with three million bikes. People of all ages ride bikes, most of which are decorated with embroidered or crocheted pieces as a way of identifying ownership, since bicycles tend to look alike. Where do all the bikes go when riders reach their destination? Bicycle parking lots, of course. Imagine parking lots with thousands of bikes being watched over by one attendant, for a two-cent fee. May and I remember visiting Amsterdam in 1966 and being impressed with the hordes of commuters on bicycles. On our return visit, a decade later, the bikes were replaced by automobiles. We wonder if a similar fate awaits China.

At the present time, private cars are a rare sight in China. The streets are filled with trucks, taxis and buses. All of these vehicles are constantly honking to warn pedestrians, bike riders and cart pushers. Drivers seem to keep one hand on the wheel and one hand on the horn. This is partly a self-defense measure, for an accident with a pedestrian or cyclist automatically means that the driver's license is revoked for a year. Such a penalty could mean the loss of a job for that period. At night, all drivers turn off their lights when approaching another vehicle, so that one has a rather ghostly feeling of objects passing in the dark. Inside our bus, we hear the constant beeping of the horn and the ding-a-ling of the bikes, all of which make the city's streets a lively and noisy place. One other interesting note about drivers of motorized vehicles: as part of the test for obtaining a license, each driver is required to be able to repair his or her vehicle. And such repairs are done on the spot. There is no such thing as a tow truck to take away the malfunctioning car to a repair shop.

People wearing white, surgical-type masks are another frequent sight in the streets of China. At first we thought these masks, covering the nose and mouth, were for the purpose of braving the chilly winds. Actually, persons wearing masks have a cold and are seeking to avoid communicating their ailment to others. That seems like a good idea, and I wondered why we haven't adopted this practice in our own country.

Another unusual scene, observable in Nanjing and other cities, is a small but vanishing number of little old ladies in their sixties and seventies with tiny, bound feet (perhaps three or four inches), shuffling along the streets. We watched with concern one such old woman, as she scurried with a peculiar gait that was once regarded as alluring, crossing a busy street, warily dodging buses and bikes, and we wondered if her tiny steps were going to bring her to her destination. Once considered a mark of beauty, foot binding, which dates back to the 10th century, has been discarded and is now regarded as a sign of bondage.

Something that immediately caught my children's attention was the constant spitting in the streets. Why the Chinese are such inveterate spitters remains a puzzle to us. My daughter Michele calls this practice "gross." "No Spitting" signs abound, and so do spittoons. But these reminders do not curb the habit. We finally decide that it is a bad habit that is difficult to eradicate. In trying to explain the persistence of this habit, one explanation is that handkerchiefs are a luxury item in China due to the shortage of cotton goods. For the most part, paper tissue is also too dear. We are accustomed to walks around the city's streets on the assumption that the best way to know a city is to walk its streets. In most cities in the West, one must cultivate the art of dodging canine droppings. At least here in China that is not a problem, for exceedingly few dogs are found in urban areas. However, one must learn to avoid stepping on "lungers."

While we are on the subject of bad habits, never have we seen so many people smoke so much as in China. It seems as if most men are heavy smokers, but very few women smoke in public. Whenever we visit a factory, office, or commune, it is customary to serve us hot tea and to pass around cigarettes in the meeting rooms for our briefing. Yes, the Chinese with whom we spoke are familiar with the U.S. Surgeon General's report on the hazards of smoking. Two reasons were frequently mentioned for the persistence of this habit: (1) It's one of the few sources of pleasure that can be enjoyed, and (2) anytime that anyone wishes to smoke, that person may take a rest from work. China does not have the institution of the "coffee break," but its equivalent seems to be the "smoke break." Since several people in our traveling group were allergic to cigarette smoke, we were all grateful for the fact that every one of our tour guides and bus drivers refrained from smoking to accommodate us. After leaving China, we learned that a nationwide campaign is now under way to curb the smoking habit. This campaign is armed with anti-smoking slogans, "No Smoking" signs in offices and factories, and even a candy substitute to help people give up smoking. Apparently the candy has the effect of making cigarette smoking unpleasant. Perhaps now the tide will turn away from the popularity of smoking. Who knows? Earlier campaigns against the "Four Pests"—not to be confused with the Gang of Four—flies, rats, mosquitoes, and sparrows, were quite successful in purging all but the irrepressible sparrows! Moreover, the chain-smoking Chairman Mao is no longer around to emulate. I wonder how he would have reacted to an anti-smoking campaign.

One familiar old sight that has completely vanished from the streets of China is the rickshaw that used to be pulled by coolies. When I was growing up in the 40s, a movie about China without a rickshaw transporting the hero and heroine was simply incomplete. In present-day China, rickshaws are inconsistent with human dignity. You can still ride in a rickshaw in the streets of Honolulu, but not in China.

Something else that has vanished: In pre-Liberation days, it was common to see streetwalkers plying their trade. Prostitutes no longer operate in the streets of China. When we were in Beijing, we did hear about the Peace Café, a hangout for younger, avant-garde types, where prostitutes gather. Their clientele consisted largely of foreign students, particularly from Third World countries. After leaving China, we heard reports that the government was embarrassed by the "gang of male and female hooligans who have corrupted the reputation of China," and had arrested sixteen prostitutes and their pimps at the Peace Café.

One final street vignette: In the six cities we have thus far visited, only two beggars have been encountered. The streets of old China, of course, were filled with many beggars, for whom begging had become a way of life. One beggar we saw was a blind man, clinging to the arms of a woman at the train station in Guangzhou; the other was a young man, perhaps recently returned from the countryside, in Nanjing. Apparently begging for money is now forbidden and is not really necessary for one's survival. However, as was indeed the actual case, three sympathetic and well-meaning members of an Overseas Chinese tour group handed out more money in a few minutes to a beggar than he would be able to earn working legitimately for an entire week. With odds like that, some will resort to begging. Today there are far fewer beggars in all of the streets of China than in the city of Detroit or New York.

November 27. Visit to a Nanjing Primary School

At our request, we spent a fascinating morning at a Nanjing primary school. We had heard that many changes are going on in China's educational system, such as the restoration of competitive entrance exams in secondary and university education, and a new intensity in learning. What better way to get a glimpse at the new learning than to start with the primary school.

As we arrived at the school gate, we were met by a delegation which consisted of the principal, a teacher, and two of the top students of the third grade. After exchanging handshakes, they ushered us into a multipurpose room, where a nicely set table with the customary hot tea was waiting. A small upright piano, a large painting of four children, each representing a different race and holding hands against the background of a map of the world, and chairs were the only furnishings in the room.

Ms. Li, the principal, extended warm greetings to the "friends from America" and then gave a background briefing. Each student has an annual health examination. Entry is at the age of six and graduates are normally eleven years old—comparable to kindergarten through sixth grade in the U.S. Before graduation, all pupils must take examinations for the Middle School. Based on this exam, students are divided into an advanced group and a regular group.

There is a fee of three yuan per three months' term (about $2.00) for primary school, whereas the charge for middle school is ten yuan per term (or $6.66). Students must purchase their own books, which cost one yuan per term (66 cents). Ms. Li reports that university education is free; however, students pay for their housing, food and books, which average about forty to sixty yuan per month (or $26 to $40 U.S.). Just as in our country, we can see where some of the funds being saved by parents go!

Built in 1952, the site of the primary school was a contaminated pond prior to Liberation. Over forty teachers and staff members work with about a thousand students who are divided into approximately forty students per class, which is quite large by America standards. Subjects taught include Chinese and English languages, math, politics, music, physical education, art, history, and geography. English instruction begins in the third grade.

The principal spent considerable time explaining the philosophy that guides the school. Education is a means to develop three dimensions of the pupil—knowledge, physical well-being, and self-conduct; or, stated another way: mental, physical, and moral maturity. Through the learning process there are five loves that are stressed: love of the motherland, public property, people, science, and labor. Students are taught international events, political movements, and famous historical personalities.

All students are encouraged to learn and to show respect for their teachers by studying hard and being obedient. Students are also encouraged to help each other and to learn from one another.

Teachers at the school have clear-cut responsibility. They are to: (1) prepare for lessons, (2) check homework, (3) prepare and give examinations, (4) give special guidance to those in need, and (5) give lessons. Teachers are also responsible for firmly abiding by schedules, monitoring students, strengthening pupils' basic knowledge, improving their own teaching skills, and improving the quality of their lessons.

Competition among students is emphasized, as the principal explained in detail various competitive exercises and contests held within the school and among other schools. She was proud of the fact that a number of the pupils from this school placed first, second, or third in province-wide contests.

As we walked out for a visit to the classes, we noticed a poster in the front office listing the school's rules. Under "Health Hazards," Rule #5 was "No Spitting!"

A typical classroom consists of benches and desks, two blackboards (one at the front and one at the back of the room), a raised platform where the teacher stands, and pictures of Chairman Mao and Zhou Enlai above the blackboards. Left of the blackboard in front was a bulletin board with a simple instruction poster for eye exercises. All the rooms had two separate entrances, but none of the rooms had heaters. When we inquired about this, we were told the school uses portable heaters when the weather is really cold. Since they did not consider today particularly cold, all the windows and doors were opened to regulate the temperature so that the classrooms would not be colder than the air outside.

By our standards, the conditions in the classrooms were quite spartan and rudimentary. We were amazed at how simple the teaching materials and resources were, especially since education of the younger generation is being stressed. Yet all the children seem to be highly motivated to learn. And in a sense this desire for learning is more important than gobs of resources and materials. What the students were learning was far more advanced than what the average U.S. primary pupil is exposed to. For example, physiology and anatomy are taught in the fourth grade, multiplication of three digits in the third grade, and algebra, geometry and physics in the fourth and fifth grades. These are subjects which my ninth grade daughter has yet to tackle in the U.S.!

Any American teacher would envy the order, decorum and obedience we saw in these classrooms. We might question the method of learning with its heavy emphasis upon rote memory and recitation. Whenever students wanted to speak, they raised their hands. Both teachers and students we saw seemed very enthusiastic. We noticed that many of the students were wearing red scarves or handkerchiefs around the neck. This signifies that they are members of a nationwide organization called the Young Pioneers. Some of the students also wore red stripes on their sleeves. These are marks of achievement. Thus the two students who greeted us at the entrance wore three stripes because they were at the top of their class.

In one class, we saw a boy who was obviously retarded. When we inquired we were informed that it is the teacher's responsibility to work with slow learners and help them catch up. However, a child who fails a class will be put a grade behind.

After we visited many of the classrooms, it came time for recess. As soon as the bell rang, the children made a mad dash into the yard. Most of the children played together in small groups. What we found fascinating was that everything the children played with (aside from basketball and ping-pong) was handmade by themselves. For example, there were small beanbags used to play a game that resembled dodge-ball, feather-kickers (with bolts and feathers), ropes for jumping, etc. Those not engaged in play things danced with each other and invited us to join them. The teachers on yard duty wore red armbands.

As soon as the bell rang, signifying the end of recess, all the children ran quickly to their rooms. Then music was piped over the loudspeaker, and it was time for eye exercises. Once a day the students have regular eye-strengthening exercises. These exercises are done simultaneously throughout the entire school for ten minutes. I wonder if these exercises explain why relatively few people seem to wear eyeglasses in China. In addition to daily eye exercises, students are asked to change their seats once a week, so that their eyes are properly exercised from different places in the classroom.

After the eye exercises, we were again led to the multi-purpose room, where a charming singing and dancing show was performed for us. About twenty girl students and a teacher who played the accordion did the entertaining. We were amazed at how mature the young students' voices sounded. The poise and the confidence they expressed served to make this performance memorable. After the finale, as we applauded, the girls clapped their hands and invited us to sing along with them. Then we were asked to sing a song. Our rendition of "I've Been Working on the Railroad," though spirited, sounded sorry when contrasted to the quality of the singing we had just heard from the children.

As we departed from the primary school, the children followed us outside and clapped their hands. They were still applauding when our bus pulled away. When we looked back from a distance, they were still waving at us and clapping their hands. There is no doubt that meeting the children in China is a very heartwarming experience.

By and large, we were impressed by this visit to the primary school. Our impressions are that there is more order and obedience here than would prevail in the typical American classroom. Also, there is greater emphasis on content or subject matter. One has the impression of a good grounding in math and science—perhaps more than our students receive. The curriculum is not that different, except that there is more of it and it comes earlier. Competition among the students is keen in terms of scores and achievement levels. Equipment, materials, books, resources are sparse. A fairly stiff dose of praise for the motherland, heroes of the Communist Party, and Marxist-Maoist teachings, makes me wonder if there is any such counterpart in the American educational system, and if not, how we manage to inculcate our cherished values.

More Notes on the Cultural Revolution

Earlier I made light of blaming all wrongs on the Cultural Revolution as a scapegoat. The longer I remain in China, the more people we talk with, the more I can understand what a wrenching and traumatic experience it must have been. Persons who were forced to don a duncecap and were paraded through town with mocking signs saying "Jackass" around their necks do not easily forget such humiliation. What began as a movement of moral regeneration wound up in violence.

Many hysterical young people were bent on destroying the "four olds" —old ideas, old customs, old culture, and old habits. China's "now generation" regarded anything old as bad. As a result, many precious objects of art, representing China's great legacy, were destroyed in museums, temples, libraries, and private homes. I must confess that to see such destruction angers me, for it is impossible to replace the irreplaceable.

The Cultural Revolution's impact was disruptive in nearly all sectors of life. A production manager at a factory informed me that output was seriously curtailed during this period, as workers, who were protesting disruptions of the economy in some cases, left their jobs to engage in debate and even physical clashes with the students.

Intellectuals seem to have borne the brunt of attacks upon tradition and learning. Their contributions had been downgraded as academic learning was ridiculed. Schools were closed and many teachers and scholars were sent to rural areas to work as farmhands, regardless of their specialties. As a result of having been burned badly, intellectuals even today have retreated from political concerns into abstract scholarship— ironically, the very haven that Red Guard members sought to destroy.

The main complaint of academicians nowadays is a familiar one to their colleagues in America: too many meetings to attend and committees on which to serve.

The Gang of Four apparently encouraged the Red Guard to move poorly housed families into educational facilities. This was an attempt to ease the housing shortage at the expense of education. Temples, churches, mosques, and museums were damaged, unless they came under the benevolent protection of the People's Liberation Army. In Nanjing, even a statue of the founder of modern China, Dr. Sun Yat Sen, was decapitated. In Shanghai, the widow of Sun Yat Sen had her house vandalized by the Red Guards. Old, treasured Buddhas were destroyed in temples. Foreigners were assaulted, Soviet diplomats attacked, the British embassy sacked and its chargé d'affaires beaten, and foreign correspondents warned to stay off the streets.

Perhaps the most "pernicious" impact of the Cultural Revolution is the apathy and lethargy, the failure of nerve on the part of China's middle management bureaucracy. They seem to be on dead center, waiting and watching but not yet moving with full force. Ironically enough, a movement that began with Mao's blessings to shake up the complacency and the routinization of the bureaucrats has been repudiated—only to see the complacency return in greater force.

Notes on Sexist Language and Women's Lib

The women's movement in America has firmly established the point that sexist language is a symbol of oppression. Certain Chinese terms now commonly employed seem to recognize this truism. For example, the word "tongzhi" means "comrade," and is the most appropriate form of address in speaking to every person, male or female, peasant or professor, waiter, worker or government official. The older forms of address, as Mr., Mrs., or Miss, have simply been replaced by "Tongzhi." Not bad. Why do we have such a difficult time in the English language finding such nonsexist designations?

Husbands and wives, when referring to their spouses in present-day China, use the term "airen," which means "loved one." Thus if I am speaking to someone with reference to my wife, I would say, my "airen," and May (hopefully) would say the same in discussions about me. Instead of saying "my husband" or "my wife," I find this term of endearment, "my loved one," quite charming.

Another example of nonsexist language came to my attention when I tried to reach Sui Mei Ting, the "airen" of Bishop K. H. Ting, by telephone in Nanjing. I discovered that she is not known by that name, but rather by her maiden name, Sui Mei Kuo. When we visited, she informed me that such is the practice in China.

On the subject of equality of the sexes, several items come to mind. In the old days, education was more a privilege of men, while women were trained to be gracious housewives or to be admired like "flower vases."

Women now have much more equal educational advantages. One finds men and women working side by side in factories and fields for the same amount of pay (so we are told). One of my American friends remains skeptical since everywhere she visited in China she found the women washing the laundry. Where both spouses work, as is typical, household chores are shared. In the morning between five and seven, men are usually out doing the family shopping and marketing, while their "airen" are readying the children for school. American readers may not realize that women in China have come a long way—much longer than Virginia Slims ads could envisage. Women have come from pre-Liberation days when they were born into families without parental joy, bought and sold like chattels, abused or abandoned to die in the streets, oppressed by mothers-in-law, and treated unequally in jobs and schooling. I am not saying that China today is a paradise for women's libbers, but the many strides toward equality are surely impressive.

VII

In Wuxi (Wushih)

November 28

Wuxi is one of the many beauty spots in China. Founded over two thousand years ago in Jiangsu province, the city is filled with canals and cobbled streets. Our hotel is situated on one of the city's major attractions, the beautiful Lake Tai Hu ("Big Lake"). Encircling this lake are lovely walkways and magnificently carved rock gardens.

It took us over an hour just to promenade around a section of these extensive walkways. On one side of us was the shimmering lake, punctuated only by a few small fishing boats. On the path where we walked were unusual flowers and trees of various sizes and shapes and smells. But most unusual were the myriad rock formations and stone carvings. It seems that long ago two wealthy brothers were engaged in a bit of sibling rivalry. One built a rock-garden path along the lakefront and won the admiration of many of the townsfolk. Seeing this, the other brother vowed he could do even better. So he set about to build a rock-garden path that was longer and even more intricate and picturesque in the patterns and shapes that were ingeniously hewn from the rocks.

We were told that during the springtime the area is even more beautiful, for the cherry blossoms are in bloom, ringing the lake and presenting a profusion of colors. Beauty in the spring is probably true for many places in China. For our return visit we were urged to come either in April or September.

Wuxi is a city of light industry with some 625,000 inhabitants, which is roughly the size of San Francisco's population. Wuxi is famous for its silk factories. Mulberry trees for silkworm farming are growing everywhere. Historically speaking, silk is perhaps China's most unique product. China was the first country in the world to raise silkworms and to weave fabrics of silk. Over three thousand years ago, the Chinese were already engaged in sericulture. Chinese silk was admired and coveted by the upper classes and royal courts in Asia and Europe. Centuries before the birth of Christ, silk caravans carried the prized product along the

Silk Road across Asia to the West and to the Roman Empire. In fact, at one time the Chinese were regarded as the "Seres," or the silk people.

In addition to silk and cotton factories, Wuxi has many machine-building and tool production factories. Light industries flourish here. These include flour mills, soap making, chemical processing, lathes, grinding machines, milling machines, power presses, metal cutting instruments, etc.

One of our excursions was a two-hour boat ride on Lake Tai Hu. Its 850 square miles make it one of China's largest lakes. Its water is clear and dotted by over a hundred small islands. The many trees, gardens, rock grottoes, and waterways combine to make this city a very restful and scenic place.

Another unusual place we visited is the Golden Light Pagoda. It is possible to climb all the way to the top for a commanding view of the environs. Then one can descend to the lower level and go through a passageway that leads to an extensive network of tunnels with many spaces set aside for storage and shelter. Even a movie theater and an amusement center are in these underground premises. In addition there are many display rooms which exhibit figurines, sculptured objects, paintings, and stone carvings. Some are for sale. We already have been introduced to Beijing's underground city. Well, here is another such place with over a hundred tunnels connected to this underground hub with its many evacuation points known to the citizenry.

Now we have seen two subterranean facilities—one in a large city, the other in a smaller one. I am told that most cities throughout north, northwest, and central China have similar facilities. Are these really nuclear shelters? Is it possible that the Chinese have some ominous prefiguration of the future that is yet beyond our grasp? Why don't we sense the same sort of danger? Do they know something we do not know? Or, alternatively, is this a harbinger of the future city? By a slight stretch of the imagination, from what we have seen of underground possibilities, perhaps the city of tomorrow, instead of being filled with skyscrapers, will consist of (for want of a better term) "groundscrapers."

November 29. Visit to Silk Factory

A trip to Wuxi would be incomplete without visiting the Number One Silk Filature Factory. For a neophyte like myself, it was quite an experience to see fine raw silk threads being packaged for export as the culmination of a process that began in another section of the plant where hundreds of young women were sorting out cocoons by hand.

For fifteen hundred years, Wuxi has been a center for breeding silkworms. This particular factory was started in 1959 and currently employs 1,800 workers, 80% of whom are women. Prior to 1949, its annual output of silk was 40 tons; now it is 390 tons, 60% of which is exported, chiefly to Japan and Western Europe. We were shown the improvements and technological innovations, particularly the semi-automated machines that enable one worker to tend sixty threads of silk simultaneously. Before the new machines, it was possible to tend only five threads.

Dramatic progress has been made during the past three decades. The factory operates its own clinic and kindergarten. Workers earn an average wage of 60 yuan per month with the lowest-paid person receiving 36 and the highest-paid 90. On the bulletin board were photographs of ten workers who merit awards of distinction and bonuses. These awards are based on output, skill, and quality of production.

The factory also conducts a primary school and a high school which meets twice a week during after-work hours on a volunteer basis. We were informed that since educational standards were so low and people learned so little during the period of the Cultural Revolution, many workers now felt the need for additional educational opportunities.

Near the end of our visit on our way out to the bus, my daughter Wendy spontaneously asked our guide if we could be shown the kindergarten. We were immediately taken down the block to an upstairs building where about a hundred children were divided into five classrooms with a teacher for each class. As we entered the first classroom, we were met by a squeal of about twenty surprised children who had been playing a game. The teacher summoned the children to order, and each one immediately went directly to his or her own chair. Then she instructed them to do a folk dance, which imitates the waddling of a duck, as she went over to the small, portable piano and began playing.

One child started the dance, waddled about, and then turned and pointed to a second child, who placed her hands on the shoulders of the first child, and followed his waddling motions. On and on went the dance until a serpentine line of all the children was formed. It was one of the most delightful, amusing, and captivating scenes one could ever expect to encounter. We too were invited to join the dance. The juxtaposition of waddling adults with five-year-olds was just hilarious and cracked us all up—or should I say quacked us up? A sense of gaiety and sheer joy was in the air. With children so happy and delightful, the future of China, come what may, can't be all that bad. We left the No. One Silk Factory with the laughter and smiles of the pre-school children very much on our consciousness. Despite our fatigue, every one of us had a smile on our lips. We can never forget those children!

This brief and spontaneous visit to a factory-sponsored kindergarten is a vivid reminder that day-care centers, nursery schools, and kindergartens are marvelously developed institutions in China. I dare say we have much to learn in America from the Chinese who work in these pre-school centers.

*
* *

In Wuxi we also visited a clay figurine studio. Wuxi is famed for its perfection of the art of clay figurines. The studio employs 600 workers, 70% of whom were women. Average salary is 45 yuan with a range from 35 to 80. Clay potters have a long tradition in China. Raw materials for their work are found in nearby fields. Before Liberation, artisans were called "clay beggars," because they had to beg people to buy their wares. Most of the products made in this studio are consumed domestically. We were impressed by the very bright colors painted painstakingly by hand on the clay figurines. Some three hundred varieties of figurines are produced in this studio. The miniature clay figurines are popular souvenirs among tourists. We too troop to the friendly store on the premises to purchase the products, largely because they will remind us of the intricate and delicate artistry which we encountered here.

Notes on a New Wind Blowing

This evening I happened to pick up from the magazine rack on our floor of the hotel the November 23, 1979, issue of the *Beijing Review*. This magazine, along with another one called *China Reconstructs,* provides much information about present-day developments in China. I must subscribe immediately to both journals.

Two items caught my attention in the *Beijing Review*. The first is an announcement that China has sent scholars and students for advanced study and research to the following countries: 500 to the U.S., 300 to Britain, 200 each to France and Germany, and 100 to Japan. This item caught my attention because at one of the factories we visited two engineers approached me for help to study abroad. They have been approved by their plant and by the government with a promise to pay all expenses, but they have yet to hear from the prospective American and Canadian institutions. They have been waiting for over a year now. I told them that a theological seminary where I teach has little influence with an engineering faculty, but I would try!

The other item was an article entitled "Correct Approach to Marxism" and cited Chairman Mao as example: "Comrade Mao Zedong, who persevered in seeking truth from facts and proceeded from reality in everything, combined the fundamental realities of Marxism-Leninism with the reality of the Chinese revolution and applied and developed Marxism in the light of actual conditions in China." The article cites this as "the genuine Marxist-Leninist approach, in contrast with mechanically made use of passages from Marx-Lenin classics in a wholesale way." It ended with a call to "seek truth from facts and link theory with practice . . . do away with blind faith and emancipate our minds."

These passages reflect a refreshingly new spirit of openness. It is different from the earlier Mao accent on "the East wind prevailing over the West wind." Perhaps a new wind is blowing fresh breezes. What an appropriate note for our visit to our next city—Shanghai.

VIII

In Shanghai

November 29

We are now in the great city of Shanghai, which maintains a friendly rivalry with Beijing as to which is the first or second city in China—much as New York and Chicago vie for comparable honors. I came to Shanghai with an air of great expectations, for I've heard so much about the city's history and have come across endless bad jokes about being "Shanghaied."

By all odds, Shanghai is the most Western of China's cities. Its high-rise office buldings, as one scans the city's skyline, give it the unmistakable appearance of London's "City Financial Area," Fleet Street, and the Thames Embankment. All of us on the bus comment on how European the city looks. One of three municipalities under the direct jurisdiction of the central government (others being Beijing and Tianjin or Tientsin), Shanghai's population of 11 million makes it the world's largest city. Since one-half of all exports pass through the port of Shanghai, it is one of China's major seaports. Already by the 18th century, Shanghai was a thriving foreign-trade center. Today it is a bustling metropolis with over eight thousand factories and an industrial work force numbering in excess of two million.

Shanghai evokes historical memories of one of China's most humiliating moments as well as one of its proudest. The latter was the founding of the Communist Party and its First National Congress held on July 1, 1921, in Shanghai. Mao Zedong was among its founders. Zhou Enlai once led a general strike and uprising here in 1927 that was temporarily successful. These facts give Shanghai the distinction of being regarded as a "revolutionary city," which continues to be its image today.

One of the darkest moments in modern Chinese history was the shelling of Shanghai and its fall to the British Navy in 1842. The British demanded an open port so they could ply their profitable and nefarious opium trade. By force of gunboats, the British, later joined by the French and Americans, gained extraterritorial rights. These foreign powers carved up Shanghai into three concessionary sections over which they ruled.

Along the waterfront street, formerly called the Bund, are located the old British quarters, the French quarters, and the American quarters. Each of these foreign sectors put up its own Western-style commercial buildings, ruled the city politically, and had a monopoly on foreign trade. They controlled banks, customs, trading houses, shipping and industry. For a full century prior to 1949's Liberation, gunboats belonging to foreign powers dominated the port and cruised up and down the river as an ominous reminder of outside control. Imagine how Americans would feel if a big chunk of New York City were in the hands of Russians, Germans and the French and their warships ruled the harbor!

Foreigners not only made Shanghai a lucrative trading center, but they imported vices that turned Shanghai into one of the world's most notorious cities of ill repute. Sailors from all over the world poured into the open port for unsavory recreation. Shanghai came to be known as a center of prostitution, opium, drugs, and gambling. The figures vary, but one estimate indicates that there were over eight hundred houses of prostitution and more than thirty thousand registered prostitutes operating in Shanghai. The street that quartered the main red-light district has been renamed "Liberation Lane." Of course, after Liberation, prostitution, drugs, and gambling have vanished. Shanghai has become a sedate city.

Foreigners reveled and reaped riches. Many lived in luxurious mansions and had companies of servants to do their bidding. It is reported that in the 1880s one wealthy British landlord named Sassoon owned 1,900 pieces of Shanghai real estate. Meanwhile, millions of Chinese were suffering from poverty and squalor just a stone's throw from the palaces and elegant homes occupied by foreigners. In a single day in the winter of 1947 dead bodies numbering 1,300 were collected from the streets of Shanghai, for the poor lacked shelter and food for survival.

To contrast those conditions with Shanghai today is a moving experience. One of our memorable visits was to the Huangpu Park on the banks of the Huangpu River, formerly known as Whangpoo. We arrived at seven a.m., but from the early hours of six a.m. to eight, hundreds of elderly Chinese men and women were engaged in daily *taijiquan* exercises. Incidentally, in every city we visited, groups of people doing their taijiquan exercises were a familiar sight. These groups range in number from ten to three hundred and follow a leader who gives instructions. There are groups for beginners and for more advanced participants. Occasionally on the crowded sidewalk of any city, a solitary person will be going through the taiji paces. Not far from the entrance to Huangpu Park, we watched various groups go through their rhythmic movements. It seemed graceful, almost like ballet dancers, rather than martial or combative.

Inside the park, a bit of anger welled up within, when I realized that from 1868 until 1928—for fully sixty years—a sign hung over the entrance that read: "Dogs and Chinese Not Allowed." Was this designed to add insult to injury? Now the Huangpu Park is open to all, Chinese and Caucasians alike, for viewing the river, filled this morning with freighters rather than warships, for the elderly to do their morning exercises, and for young courting couples.

Across the street from the park, we visited what was formerly the British consulate. It has been converted into a Friendship Store. For China's sake, I am delighted that the era of colonialism is a thing of the past. Its people have suffered enough from the humiliation and exploitation of rapacious foreign traders.

From the Friendship Store, we move to another formerly famous landmark: the elegant racetrack for sporting fans to place their bets. Today the old racetrack has been converted into a beautiful People's Park with gardens, shady trees, and decorative rocks. The old Race Club now houses the 6.2-million-volume Shanghai Library. Where the gamblers once placed their bets is now the main Library Reading Room. Horse racing has been supplanted by edification of the mind!

In present-day Shanghai, one has the impression of greater prosperity, of more diversity in dress, colors and hair styles. The women seem more attractive and more conscious of their appearance. Young couples are seen, more than in any other city, holding hands or walking arm in arm in the streets, and in affectionate embraces in the parks. The Peace Hotel (formerly called the Palace and owned by Sassoon) is similar to the Beijing Hotel as the gathering place for foreigners, who give the place an international ambiance. Shanghai is no longer open in the raunchy sense. It remains an open city in the sense of welcoming new winds of change and innovation.

Our first evening in Shanghai, we attended a ballet. Again, the show contained no propaganda, no military music or proletarian hero. It was strictly a modern ballet, employing dazzling stage settings. The ballet was based on a classical fairy tale. Love and romance were featured prominently. Predictably, the hero was dressed in white and the villain had black attire. Many references were made to heaven. Indeed, both hero and heroine die a tragic death and are whisked away to heaven, Peter Pan style, amid generous puffs of white clouds floating onto the stage. At the climax, the villain is slain by an arrow which is thrown by the hero with his last gasp of strength. Then the hero goes off to join his beloved in heaven. Although there are comical portions, the ballet is really a musical tragedy, staged in a charming and entertaining style. Its costumes and stage sets are impressive. However, we have seen smoother and more graceful ballet dancing, especially at transition points and where balance is essential. Note the recovery of such themes as love and romance and heaven, as classical stories are making their return to the theater.

It seems that every performance in every theater we have attended was jam-packed, standing room only. When I inquired, it was explained to me that tickets are allocated to communes and factories and work teams for popular distribution among those who wish to attend a certain performance. An effort is made to have workers and peasants attend cultural events.

Even if people are not provided with admission tickets, the price for admission is quite modest—about five cents. As we related earlier, money is not the major problem in China. A working couple can live quite adequately and have funds for theatrical events. The problem is finding enough consumer products to purchase, given the coupon system of rationing goods. Thus ballet, movies, acrobatic shows and opera are very well attended. I don't remember seeing any empty seats. Some of the auditoriums we went to were drafty and even downright cold. After shivering through one performance, I always dressed warmly on the grounds that it is easier to shed excess clothing than to shiver.

November 30. Notes on Response to Democracy Wall

On our second day in Shanghai, I was dismayed to hear a report from a member of the Communist Party with whom I was conversing at a factory that the People's Congress had just passed a resolution rescinding the use of Democracy Wall in Beijing. When I asked him why, he replied that the notices on the Wall were undermining the government's four modernization goals, that they were sabotaging attempts to unify the people, and that they constituted a threat against the socialist system.

I countered by saying that I had seen the wall posters, that they spoke essentially of grievances against bureaucratic bungling or abuses of officials and police, and not against the socialist system as such. Therefore, its impact is to cleanse the system and strengthen it, rather than to undermine it.

It became apparent that the more we conversed, the more our different backgrounds and biases surfaced. He wanted to remain loyal to his government, whose directives he believes and seeks to follow implicitly, whereas I expressed my proclivity for healthy skepticism towards political power brokers, and a preference for criticism. After all, had not the People's Congress favored "emancipation of the mind" and "seeking the truth from facts"? He admitted these policies are now being advocated by the top leaders.

Our discussion was left at this ambiguous impasse. I confess to a personal disappointment at the closing of Democracy Wall. Perhaps this is a signal that limits to liberty must be set. Or perhaps there is concern that the Gang of Four still has its network of supporters. The Wei Jingshen arrest and sentencing for fifteen years, so widely reported in Western

journals, may have sent shock waves that created the crackdown on dis-
senters. It is clear that dissenting groups do exist, and how to deal with
them remains a divisive issue.

In a dialogue published in the Communist Party newspaper, *The
People's Daily*, one of the disputants argued: "If somebody expresses
counter-revolutionary ideas, you should use revolutionary ideas to debate with him—but don't go and arrest him." This sort of sentiment indicates the degree of uneasiness within official circles. I suspect that
despite the new spirit of openness there is considerable anxiety about
raising fundamental questions that challenge the nature of the socialist
system.

Notes on Delinquent Youth and Crime in the Streets

In large cities, such as Shanghai, a small but unruly minority of young
people have begun disorderly behavior, fighting in gangs, and disrupt-
ing the tranquillity of the community. These young people are idle and
restless. Many are jobless, having recently returned from the countryside, where they were sent during the Cultural Revolution. They have
not yet been relocated. Hence it is estimated that perhaps ten to twenty
million unemployed young people live in the cities.

In a recent *Beijing Review* article, the subject of reformatories for
delinquent youth is dealt with. Ten such schools exist in Beijing for
1,423 students who were committed for such offenses as "fisticuffs, petty
larceny, or hooliganism."

I have no way of knowing just how serious the wayward youth problem has become. We did talk to a retired worker who said that his street
committee, consisting largely of retired folks, was assigned the task of
keeping an eye on the youth, on the assumption that if young people
know that they are being watched, they will be less inclined to engage in
wanton behavior. Also they know they will be held responsible for their
misdeeds.

I can't help thinking that the youth problems in the big cities are curi-
ously related to the shut-down at Democracy Wall. Disorderly conduct
of young people is a horrible reminder of the dissent run amuck during
the dismal days of the Cultural Revolution! There seems to be an odd
logic at work that relates free expression to dissent, dissent to disorder,
and disorder to rebellion against the socialist system.

Every society must carry out a delicate balance between freedom and
order, lest anarchy reign. For China at this juncture in history, stability
is so necessary, if confidence is to be restored and the four goals of modernization are to be sought.

One further reflection: The current news about crime and delinquency in China is startling because only a few years ago, reports circulated that street crimes and muggings had been eradicated. Even though
criminal behavior, robbing, pickpocketing, have now become a reality,

we must be careful not to exaggerate the picture. It is only a tiny fraction of the amount of crime committed in the typical large American city. Welcome to the club!

November 30. A Glimpse at Shanghai's Industrial Might

We took an early morning stroll on Nanjing Road, so named as a reminder of the infamous Treaty of Nanjing, signed with the British in 1842. This walk is intended to prepare us for what we know will be a full day visiting industrial machinery places. In other cities in China, we were amazed at how relatively few stores there were for shopping, given the size of the population. This is not the case with Nanjing Road, which has plenty of shops and store windows with attractive decorations to promote the goods for sale inside. I'm afraid our walk and window shopping took us too far afield, for when May and I returned to the hotel for breakfast, the others had nearly finished, and we endured the taunts of our fellow travelers—"Chee law, Chee law," which obviously means "late, late."

Our first exposure to the industrial might of Shanghai was a trip to the Shanghai Industrial Exhibition. The Exhibition is housed in several huge halls built in the mammoth architectural style of the Soviet Union. Indeed, during an earlier period of mutual admiration, the building had been known as the Sino-Soviet People's Friendship Center. Now it is a permanent display of Chinese industrial products, most of which are produced in Shanghai. Several engineers and business types in our group were fascinated by all the modern equipment being shown. Just about anything you can imagine in the modern world of technology is here. Computers, petrochemical products, motorized vehicles (from small trucks to limousines), shipbuilding, iron and steel production, oil refining, electrical equipment, glassware, chemicals, paper production, tires, tractors, textiles, metallurgy, handicrafts, turbo-generators, precision tools, grinding machines, welding techniques, graphic arts, etc. You name it, it's there. We kept wondering to ourselves: these modern machines and technological products are here, but why don't we see more of them in the society at large? Perhaps the point of this exhibition hall is to show China's productive potential. Or perhaps Shanghai is that avant-garde city where it is only appropriate to show a glimpse of tomorrow today. I must confess that all these consumer products on display in section after section and building after building seemed a bit much when contrasted to the simple, austere life we had become accustomed to seeing throughout China.

At the Shanghai Machine Tools and Precision Instruments Plant

I could not help thinking, another day, another factory. At the gate leading to the Shanghai Machine Tools and Precision Instruments Plant we were greeted by no fewer than five applauding senior staff members and by a welcoming sign made especially for our group's visit. What a surprise!

This huge plant employs six thousand workers. In the reception room, we were told that prior to Liberation, this plant produced only crude hoes for tilling the soil. Today it manufactures over three hundred different kinds of precision grinding machines. These machines were formerly imported from abroad. Now, in addition to serving a domestic market, this plant exports its products to forty countries, including the United States and Canada.

The factory is organized into eighteen departments and eight workshops. We had time only to visit two of the workshops. The director of technical services, the secretary to the president, two senior engineers, and another staff officer escorted us. Three of them spoke English quite well and scattered themselves among us. Several members of our group with backgrounds in engineering and computers found the set-up fascinating and raised all sorts of technical questions. It became apparent that this is a well-managed, model plant which engages in producing sophisticated instruments. At one point we had to don smocks and replace our shoes with slippers to ensure that we carried no dust into the production room.

I discovered that the factory operates three schools which workers may attend during after-work hours. These schools are to equip employees in general subjects as well as technical ones. We toured the hospital in the plant where both treatment and convalescent facilities are available. We saw, among other things, an acupuncturist and a dentist at work, a woman worker recuperating from burns she suffered on the job and spending time knitting in bed, and a male patient with a splint on his leg. I was interested to learn that the medical staff does not simply stay at the hospital, but once a week a doctor visits on location each of the eight workshops. This roving physician confers with the workers on the state of their health and whether there are any problems, and keeps an eye on prevention of sickness. These conferences are held right on the spot with either one or a group of workers clustered around the doctor. Smart idea!

For me and my daughters, the most engaging part of our visit to this industrial plant was the nursery school and kindergarten it sponsors. Again, my daughter Wendy, who loves children, asked our guide if we could possibly visit the pre-school facilities. Immediately we were taken there by bus. We approached a row of perhaps a half-dozen freshly painted white bungalows specially built at the far end of the plant.

We were introduced to a very impressive setting: modern, well-equipped, bright facilities with audio and visual materials, blackboards and supplies of all types for fun and learning. Worker-mothers come to visit their babies and feed them in the nursery school once in the morning and once in the afternoon. When we arrived unannounced, the feeding period had just ended, and the proud mothers held their babies up high for us to admire. The happy babies seemed pampered by the mothers and nurses in their white uniforms. They did not seem to be bothered at all by these strange visitors marching in on them. How could this scene of contented babies and cooing mothers possibly be topped?

To my amazement, it was immediately topped when we crossed over to a series of interconnected classroom buildings. There must have been twenty classes, each clean, bright, well decorated, and filled with children who could warm even the cockles of an old Scrooge. The children sang, danced, recited poems. They invited us to dance with them. Each time we left a room to visit another one, the children sang us a farewell song with the words "Goodbye, uncles and aunties." These three- to five-year-old boys and girls—so well-behaved, well-scrubbed, and well-dressed—completely won over our hearts. As important as are grinding machines and precision tools for meeting production quotas, for enhancing China's move to modernization, and for meeting balance-of-payments problems, nothing can be more satisfying than to see the happy children of China. Now I can fully understand why China is fond of referring to her children symbolically as "blossoms of the motherland." They are a truly enchanting lot and augur well for China's future. Again, we came away feeling that there are lessons to be learned here in China's nursery schools and day-care centers which would be helpful in other parts of the world.

To leave Shanghai with the laughter of children ringing in our ears is delightful. I was further pleased to know that Shanghai is San Francisco's sister city. In spirit, there is an affinity between these two great cities. Also, the Shanghai Communiqué, signed by President Nixon and Premier Zhou on Feburary 1, 1972, will historically be remembered as the basis for a new era of relationships between China and the United States.

IX

In Hangzhou (Hangchow)

December 2

From Shanghai we board the train for the 115-mile trip to Hangzhou, the capital of Zhejiang province and home for one million inhabitants. I was eager to see Hangzhou to find out whether it conformed to the image of beauty that was communicated to me by my good friend and mentor, Robert E. Fitch, former Professor of Ethics and Dean at the Pacific School of Religion in Berkeley. Hangzhou is the birthplace of Fitch, the community of his boyhood memories.

I'm sure Bob would feel right at home, playing in the lake and dashing around the pathways. I even asked an old-timer, a semi-retired Chinese minister in his seventies, if he knew the name Fitch. His eyes brightened as he said, "Oh yes—there was a Fitch who led the choir in which I sang as a boy!" In fact, he told me that the old missionary quarters where the Fitch family lived had been turned into a "Children's Palace," which is a learning and play center for children. Bob Fitch agreed that this is an excellent usage of his old domicile.

Bob is correct! Hangzhou is a city of breathtaking scenic beauty. In China, this city has the reputation of being the earthly equivalent of a heavenly paradise. Once called "the Celestial City," the early foreign sojourner Marco Polo referred to Hangzhou as "meriting preeminence to all other cities in the world, by its grandeur and beauty, as well as its abundant delights, which might lead one to imagine himself in Paradise." Our hotel faces West Lake, which is bound to be one of the world's beauty spots. West Lake is bordered by hills on three sides. Around the lake are situated many well-tended botanical gardens, rock grottoes, and fountains.

We walked around the lake, passing over gently sloping bridges under which hundreds of large golden carp congregated and broke the surface with puckered lips to snatch floating bits of breadcrumbs. An ideal place for honeymooners! Around the lake, the causeways, bridges, and small pavilions have created the type of scenery so frequently captured in Chinese paintings.

Drooping willow trees, lining both sides of the city's streets, add further charm. Due to its lakes and parks, trees and flowers, rocks and hills, Hangzhou gives the appearance of a resort community. Actually, the city is engaged in considerable industry—especially chemicals, fertilizer, silk and machine tools. Bordering the city are vast fields of tea plants, which provide their own picturesque scene.

Hangzhou is famous for its Dragon Well Tea (Long Jing), which is grown by the tea commune. A choice can be made among many grades and aromas that are available. Famed among tea connoisseurs for 1,300 years, Long Jing is commonly said to be green in color, fragrant in smell, mellow in taste, and elegant in shape.

As we strolled along the lake, we looked across to a villa where Richard Nixon and Zhou Enlai worked out the historically significant agreement that later became known as the Shanghai Communiqué. I suppose I should be grateful to Nixon for this achievement, since normalization of relationships has made possible our journey. Everywhere we went in China, we discovered that Nixon is regarded as a hero and a great friend. Ironic that the man who first earned his political stripes as an anti-Communist battler should end his career more loved by this Communist nation than in his own land! If Nixon should tire of San Clemente or New York or wherever, I'm sure he will always find a hospitable home in China.

Our boat ride on West Lake and our visits to Hangzhou's parks, gardens and pagoda-roofed pavilions make this a very restful city for the weary traveler. These relaxing moments gave us comfort and rest to recover from respiratory ailments, which spared no one in our group.

December 3. Visit to the Temple of Yue Fei

We had an interesting visit to the Temple of Yue Fei and his tomb, for this visit links ancient history with contemporary events. Yue Fei was a 12th century popular general, much loved by the people. He was very loyal to the emperor during the Song dynasty (960–1280). In fact, he was the only leader capable of rallying troops to defend the area time after time against the pesty invaders known as troops of the Nuchen nobles of northwestern China.

There stands a large statue of our hero the general in the main building. Nearby on the wall are the inscriptions, written in classical Chinese calligraphy: "Dedicate Your Life to the Motherland." For almost a millenium, the people had come to pay their respects to this statue and to draw inspiration from the inscription.

During the Cultural Revolution, this beloved statue of Yue Fei (about the size of Lincoln's figure at the Lincoln Memorial) was smashed to bits and the inscription totally defaced. General Yue Fei had become a victim of the iconoclastic Red Guards. The Gang of Four had decreed that Yue Fei should no longer be regarded as a hero, but as a tool of feudal society. Since the inscription referred to a feudal emperor, one should not dedicate one's life to such a motherland.

Despite the pleas of Zhou Enlai to preserve the temple and tomb as a historic relic, the place was wrecked, along with many priceless stone tablets with ancient artistic calligraphy, which the Chinese admire so much. These tablets were nearly a thousand years old. Even now we could see they were defaced, many sections chipped away, or phrases blotted out.

The government has recently spent $400,000 for restoring the large statue of the general and for rebuilding the temple, which was reopened in October, 1979, after having been closed for twelve years. When we visited, it was evident that some of the destruction was irreplaceable.

Ironically enough, at the age of 39, General Yue Fei was murdered by a conspiracy of three men and one woman, who were jealous of his position in the court and his favor with the people. One might suspect that this was a contrived story. But the clear-cut evidence is there. Long before there was such a thing as the Cultural Revolution (or even the Communist Party of China), in the same temple grounds, four copper statues, showing the execution of these four betrayers, had been erected. Through the centuries, the common people would come to this corner of the temple and spit or even urinate at this ancient "Gang of Four."

With the overthrow of the current Gang of Four and the revelation of their misdeeds, you can well imagine that ridicule and hostility toward these four figures of copper continue to be vented today. Indeed, a prominent sign reminds the populace to "Keep the Area Clean. It Is Unhealthy to Spit or to Urinate in Public!" Even so, we saw people right in front of us slapping and spitting at the four villains.

On our way back to the bus, my daughter Wendy asked, "Dad, how could the Gang of Four stay in power so long, if what they did was so bad and against the will of the people?" A good question! I wish I knew why wrong often sits on the throne of power.

Doubtless we are still too close to this period for a definitive history of the Cultural Revolution to be written. One also wonders if the internal intrigues and power struggles will ever be fully revealed. After all, China does not have the kind of investigative reporting for which the *Washington Post* is noted. If only Chairman Mao or Premier Zhou could have written their memoirs—as our former president and illustrious ex–secretaries of state are wont to do. If the main architect of current policies, Vice Premier Deng, were to write what he knows and has experienced, what fantastic insights would surface! Alas, that is not the way things are done in China. In fact, it is only in very recent presidential administrations in our own country that such memoirs, which yield lucrative financial rewards, no longer appear unseemly and unscrupulous. I wonder myself about such profiteering. Shouldn't Nixon, Ford, and Kissinger contribute these gains to projects that enhance the national welfare?

I still felt uneasy about being unable to give my inquiring daughter a good answer. Later on, when we returned to the subject, I told her that there was speculation that Chairman Mao was in very poor health and vulnerable during the last decade of his life. His wife, Jiang Qing, the female member of the Gang of Four, became very powerful and maneuvered some of her own supportes into positions of power and authority. They exercised control over many areas of life, including drama, film, the arts and mass communication, newspapers and education. Certain cities, such as Shanghai and Nanjing, were strongholds of the Gang. Fortunately, the People's Liberation Army did not come under the Gang's influence.

Another plausible explanation claims that Mao was actually declining in influence, losing his grip over the Party professionals, who were about to disregard him or even dislodge him. He therefore sparked a "children's crusade" to reform lagging ideological commitment and to reassert his own power over against the entrenched bureaucracy. He even risked destroying the Party structure in order to rebuild loyalty to his flagging revolutionary leadership. According to this viewpoint, Chairman Mao sought to clothe his dwindling power with the figleaf of the Cultural Revolution.

Still another theory explains the Cultural Revolution not in terms of personality clashes and power struggles, but rather as an attempt to recover the Maoist vision for a China headed toward a wayward path. Deliberate confusion and chaos were unleashed to shake up established and settled ways, to learn through shock methods, to afflict the comfortable, to break up bureaucratic rigidity, to reorder thought and rededicate lives to Maoist fundamentals. At some point in the struggle, however, chaos went too far—rumors fed on rumors, violence bred more violence, until order had to be restored, sometimes by force of the People's Liberation Army, and also by sending young activists to the countryside.

Whatever the explanation, one thing is clear. Chairman Mao was obviously an exceedingly complex personality. No doubt he was a great leader who has left his giant imprint upon the sands of 20th-century world history. It was Mao who led an ailing nation to rediscover its grandeur, its sense of national identity and purpose. He was a poet of revolution who frequently cited classical poets and scholars from China's ancient dynasties. Yet this same visionary had a petulant side to his personality. He could be terribly humble (referring to himself as only a lone monk walking the world with a leaky umbrella), yet insufferably arrogant, fickle and ruthless in dealing with foe and friend alike. He could identify with the peasants and yet strike out for personal immortality. He could express disdain for thinking and schooling ("A little reading of books is all right, but a lot of it harms people; it really harms them!"); yet his thoughts and his teachings were inculcated into the minds of the Chinese masses by little red books and other writings. Indeed, Mao prided himself as first and foremost a teacher.

At the end of the day, I must confess that it still remains a mystery why such a traumatic madness as the Cultural Revolution was unleashed. It would be an irony of history if all the commotion instigated by Mao, and now blamed on the Gang of Four, was indeed stirred up by an aging soldier-revolutionary who refused to fade away. Who knows for sure?

December 4. Notes on Retirement Celebrations

This is the fourth city we have visited where our attention was captured by clanging cymbals and blaring horns emanating from a brightly decorated truck speeding its way through the center of town. What we are witnessing is a sort of rite of passage. A person's retirement is being celebrated with festive noises.

It usually begins at the workplace, where speeches are given, recognition awards or scrolls bestowed, and small gifts presented. The lion dances in cadence with beating drums and roaring firecrackers. There is an air of gaiety to honor the retiree. Thus the honored guest is given a royal ride to his home in an open truck amid all the fanfare we have witnessed, as the noisy truck goes racing by. That's going out in style!

Retirement in China may come at the tender age of fifty for women and fifty-five for men, if they happen to be laborers. For those in what might be considered "white collar" jobs, the retirement age is fifty-five for women and sixty for men. A retired person continues to receive 70% to 75% of his or her last month's salary. However, a person may elect to remain on the job in many cases, either full or part time.

I wondered why people retire at such a "young" age. I mean, after all, I can foresee fifty-five not far over the hill for myself! The reason, I am told, is to make way for all the young workers coming along. Workers are assigned to jobs by the government. By retirement at age fifty-five, more people can be absorbed into the labor force. Frequently a son will step into a job vacated by his father. In an economy where labor intensity is so dominant, it is not always easy to provide employment opportunities or to match persons to job preferences.

In certain jobs, where technical skill or special training are required, or where shortages prevail, those eligible for retirement are asked to stay on. For example, we met a seventy-year-old chemistry professor who is still teaching full time.

I rather like the idea of celebrating retirements with merriment and joyful noises, clanging cymbals, firecrackers, and lion dances. It serves to confer dignity on work and the worker. Even the noise is appropriate. It calls attention to the fact that however small the contribution or menial the task, it should be recognized. It is good to affirm people in their work, not only for the retiree, but also for those who celebrate the fact. Everyone shares in the meaning and purpose of life and work. Hail and farewell! I hope to hear a lot of noise when my day of retirement comes!

*
* *

Notes on Love and Romance

Whoever claims that there is scant evidence of love and romance in China is not looking in the right places. While the Chinese are not given to exhibitions of affection in public places the way some Americans like to flaunt their eros, it is not uncommon nowadays to see couples strolling arm in arm or holding hands in the city streets. These scenes are common in Hangzhou.

My children went for a stroll to a nearby park in Beijing on a ordinary weeknight. When they returned, they gleefully reported spotting more than twenty young couples expressing their mutual affection while seated on park benches or cuddling against a small wall. My teenagers referred to these activities as "necking" and pronounced that love and romance are alive and well in China! Note that the Beijing night air in late November is not just nippy; it is downright freezing. So long as love and romance are in the air, life can't be all that drab and dull!

December 4. At the Silk Brocade Mill

Since Hangzhou is known as the silk capital, our last visit in this city was to the silk brocade mill, the Tu Chin Sheng Silk Factory. This plant produces pictures for framing and hanging on walls. It also makes tablecloths, furniture cushions and bedspreads.

Over twenty silk mills operate in Hangzhou. However, this is the only mill that produces decorative silk brocade and woven sceneries. Established in 1922, the products of this mill were formerly made by hand on looms limited to black and white color production. Since Liberation, rapid strides have been made in technological improvements. The 17 manually operated looms have been converted into 340 electrically run ones.

Workers can now weave products with fifteen different colors and over a thousand different designs. The mill employes 1,800, of which 55% are women. Employees are encouraged to innovate, to design and create more variety in patterns. Additional work space and machines are being added.

The government sets production quotas. All finished products are sent to the Hangzhou Gift Bureau, which allocates the amount for export and for domestic use. Competition between workers and among work teams is fostered, culminating in a national competitive program conducted annually in Beijing. Local, regional, and national awards are given to factories with the best products in quality and quantity. Last year, this mill won a gold prize and a silver prize in the national contest.

Like many other industrial establishments, the average wage in this mill is 60 yuan per month with the highest employee at 130 and the lowest receiving 32. The mill operates a dining room, dormitory, clinic, library and nursery school. Housing costs from three to five yuan per month.

During the Cultural Revolution, this mill was hit especially hard. Workers went on strike. They were encouraged by the Gang of Four to stop working. Those who stayed on to work were ostracized. The mill was able to meet only 30% of its production quota. There was general turmoil and disruption. All that has now been put aside, as the mill is operating smoothly at a fast production clip.

Although there is no such thing as annual vacations with pay in China, employees do get seven holidays per year with pay. These special days include National Day (like our Fourth of July), New Year's Day, Spring Festival, Worker's Day, May Day, and International Women's Day. If working couples happen to be separated, they are granted twenty days' vacation with pay to spend together. This explanation created a ripple of laughter in our group when the translator said that "two lovers who are separated can spend twenty days a year together." Such idle discussions led to questions about dalliances and assignations. Our guide insisted vehemently that no such thing as premarital or extramarital sex happens in China. "That is forbidden!" he exclaimed with a sober face. Although we met such professions of sexual purity with mock incredulity, we did have the distinct impression that China lacks the kind of blatant sexual obsession and sexplosive saturation that characterizes American society. When I asked our university-trained guide if he had ever heard of Sigmund Freud, my question was met with a blank expression of nonrecognition. I might just as well have asked if he had ever met the man in the moon.

Nearly every place we visit in China, with the exception of heavy-machinery and equipment factories, the last stop is a retail store where items may be purchased. Of course, the temptations are well-nigh irresistible at the silk brocade shop, where we all came away with exquisite brocades.

Our group has developed its own slogans. One of these, as we approach the last stopping point, is "Buy, Buy, Buy!" Of course, our guides thought that we were merely bidding farewell to the place. But even they got the idea, as our luggage grew bulkier and heavier following our departure from each city.

No wonder we attracted gawkers! Our family was carrying quite an assortment of goods that could not be packed away from city to city. My son Marcus bought a hand-pounded brass cymbal, which he slung over his shoulders. Marcus claims they just don't make cymbals in the U.S. with this tonal quality. It was, indeed, a beautiful instrument. We purchased a Beijing, four-by-eight-foot handmade wool carpet, which our children insisted we had to get to hang in our house. Marcus slung this over his ample shoulders also. Matt's carry-on bag was quite a sight. In it he had a sturdy bicycle seat (again: "they don't make them like this back home!") which must have weighed ten pounds, a leather basketball, and empty beer bottles from each city we visited to add to his strange collection, plus part of the main frame of a bicycle (which "they don't make..."). In addition, the boys carried hand-carved canes made from unusual wood with artistic knobs, and they assisted several of our older travelers by carrying their hand luggage. Matt also carried a bag filled with photo equipment, including a tripod! My daughter Mellanie carried such unusual objects as papier-mâché masks, large feather fans, rolled-up art prints, and a bottle of Mao Tai (she claimed she liked the shape of the old bottle). Speaking of which, Mao Tai (150 proof) is just about the strongest alcoholic beverage ever invented. We had a not so amusing incident when Marcus was carrying a bottle for Gloria (our tour guide from Hong Kong); somehow the bottle broke on the floor of our bus. Its fumes were so pungent that we were either going to gag or go high. Opening windows and doors didn't seem to help. The powerful smell lingered. His tote bag will never be the same—not to speak of soiled books and travelers' checks. May saw to it that neither she nor I were empty-handed either, as we lugged our goodies from place to place.

X

To Guilin (Kweilin)

December 4

In the late afternoon we leave Hangzhou by train and cross over the first indigenous suspension bridge, built by the Chinese in 1934. Looking backward, we catch a glimpse of the setting sun on West Lake with all its shimmering radiance. In the distance we gaze at the tea fields growing along terraced steps up the slopes of the mountains.

Henceforth whenever I drink Dragon Well Tea, I shall remember that each plant is carefully watered by hand, that the petals are plucked only during three days in the springtime, and that these tea leaves are picked traditionally by virgin girls with delicate hands! From the perspective of the speeding train, the carefully tended terrain appears to be manicured. Indeed, Hangzhou is aptly termed the "heavenly city."

For the next twenty-six hours, we journey on the train to Guilin. Having previously spent a difficult night on the train from Beijing to Nanjing for fourteen hours, during which there were frequent and jerky stops, loud noises from station platforms, and little chance for sound sleep, we were all girding ourselves for the ordeal. Actually, this time the ride was quite pleasant and we managed to sleep through most of the night.

During the day, we could see many small villages en route as well as fields tilled to capacity with agricultural products growing. Small children gathered to wave to us as our train passed by.

Well-rested, we arrive in Guilin in the early evening amidst a light rainfall—the first rain we have experienced since the trip started. The streets of Guilin are lined with cassia trees which exude a pleasant fragrance.

With a population of 650,000, Guilin serves as a second big city for the Guangxi Zhuang Autonomous Region in southern China. Some would rate this city as the most beautiful spot in China. With its jagged mountains and clusters of needle-like peaks rising abruptly off the ground, Guilin is indeed charming and picturesque. An artist or photographer would have a field day here, trying to capture the essence of the awesome landscape with its multi-faceted rock configurations. Here is nature in all of its raw beauty.

If Hangzhou is hailed as a "Heavenly City," precisely because of its beautiful blending of water, mountains, grottoes and gardens, how are we to speak of Guilin? For centuries, artists have sought to express an answer through their paintings rather than with words. This city provides artistic inspiration for many paintings, embroidered works, and silk brocade sceneries.

For a full day's exploration, we headed for the hills, or more precisely, the caves, which are filled with stalactites and stalagmites of all sizes and shapes. They provide a veritable Rorschach test. Millions of years of erosion by rain and underground waterways had molded the soft limestone into weird formations and fantastic grottoes.

The Seven Star Crag and the Reed Flute Caverns that we visited are especially famous for their beauty and color. These deep caverns evoke awe, as one can make out configurations that clearly resemble facets of the outside world: a camel, snake, turtle, lion, monkey, horse, eagle, giraffe, elephant, and myriad other animals. Also visible are just about all the fruits conceivable: bananas, pineapples, melons, apples, grapes, lemons, etc. Entire scenes are present: silk curtains a theater with performers on stage, a sentry standing guard, a tiered field of tea plants, a vast rain forest with dashing waterfalls, the Great Wall of China, Santa Claus, the Nativity scene of the Three Wise Men who are bearing gifts for the baby Jesus. Of course, this scene was our own interpretative imagining. The local tour guide preferred the more class-conscious, proletarian version of three peasants confronting an oppressive landlord!

In any case, it was really stunning and impressive to be in this underground world where nature has wrought such wonders for millions of years. Only the eerie squeaking of bats, hidden in the dark recesses above, made us want to leave the shadowy world of the caves and come out to the light, where vision is clearer.

By now the rains continued their downpour. We could peer but dimly beyond to the jagged mountain peaks. Even enshrouded in the dewy mist, they were of consummate beauty, standing erect and implacable, as if to proclaim that earth abides. Warring and restless humanity, plagued by competing ideologies and conflicting claims, cannot move the silent strength of these jutting peaks which reach for the sky.

The next day we spent cruising down the Li River, which wends its way in serpentine fashion through water so shallow that only a skilled boatsman can maneuver between the river rocks and the shallows. The river's banks are covered with bamboo groves and lush green shrubbery. Looking up, we marvel at the picturesque rock formations, the jagged peaks and jutting hills of all shapes and sizes and colors. One peak is so sleek it is referred to as a Chinese writing brush. Various hills are given names that reflect their shape: "Ram's Horn Hill," "Nine Horse Hill," "Brocade Hill," "Moon Hill," "Bald-headed Man Hill," etc. Other familiar shapes form in the mind's eye, as the imagination is set free: a camel, a pine forest, a mushroom, the Three Mile Island nuclear plant, etc. During lunch on the boat, I sat next to an artist who is on the staff of the Italian embassy in Beijing. He vows to return here to capture the beauties of the landscape on canvas, as generations of native artists before him have done.

Whoever said that one can love Guilin because of its clear water ponds, charming gardens, fantastic mountains, and fabulous caves has spoken the word of truth.

December 6. Notes on Hotel Accommodations

On several occasions during our travel in China, people have asked us what we thought of the hotel facilities. I usually reply that we didn't come to China for its hotels. Then I detect a frown or pained expression. One person said, "Oh, are they really that bad?" As a matter of fact, they are not bad at all. They may be rated adequate to quite good.

Recall that we did not normally stay at the very best or first-class facilities, for our less expensive reservations were at the Overseas Chinese hotels. Hence my comments do not pertain to the likes of the Beijing Hotel or the Peace Hotel in Shanghai. Nearly every place we go, we see new hotels being constructed. In fact, tourist facilities are being erected in over twenty cities, including a mammoth twenty-five-story hotel in Shanghai with accommodations for 1,000. Clearly China is building additional facilities to meet the influx of tourists.

Our friends had advised us beforehand to bring our own toilet paper and cleanser to scrub the bathtubs and sinks. However, we found that these supplies were unnecessary, for the toilet tissue was sufficiently soft and the sinks and tubs were adequately clean. Midway through the trip we were glad to save suitcase space by giving these materials away. Of course, it was handy to carry tissue paper for the public facilities where it is frequently absent.

If pressed about facilities, my remarks would center on the need for improvements in care and maintenance. We stayed in a number of hotels which were only two years old. Yet they were prematurely aged. I was puzzled by the signs of "instant aging"—cracking walls, peeling tiles and the like. It seems that energy is galvanized for constructing the buildings, and then priorities are shifted elsewhere following their erection.

Maintenance is deferred even for new buildings. Windows may be cracked or broken and remain unrepaired. Sixteen persons in our travel group occupied eight rooms. Generally speaking, two of these rooms would have showers or toilets that were malfunctioning. It was always a joke with us as to who would be stuck with those rooms. One amusing incident highlighted our bantering. My son Marcus had unpacked his clothes from his suitcase and laid his pants on the floor near his bed. In the middle of the night a leak developed from the toilet plumbing and managed to soak his clothing. Without pants to wear, he scrounged around until he found something that most nearly fit—his aunt Bettie's slacks. Dressed in this feminine apparel, he endured our taunts and even more stares from the populace than is usually the case.

Excellent handwoven Beijing wool rugs with beautiful designs (which in the U.S. retail market would sell for $1,000) were frequently on the floors of our hotel rooms; yet these rugs were badly soiled for lack of cleaning equipment. Hardwood floors were polished to a shine, but bathroom tile floors were dirty—which could easily have been remedied by a little elbow grease.

It's not so much a lack of cleaning detergents, as it is a difference in standards of cleanliness. A little training, instruction, and supervision by an alert management working with the seemingly large number of attendants who are available for duty on each floor, should go a long way in making the tile floors clean and keeping maintenance up to date. Besides, the buildings deserve that sort of tender loving care if they are to withstand the wear and tear.

When China looks at the maintenance and upkeep of hotels in Hong Kong and Taiwan, I think some changes will be made. Moreover, I shudder to imagine the coming revolution when Holiday Inn, Hilton, and Pan Am's International hotels complete construction of their facilities and begin to manage them.

To sum up: generally speaking, American travelers are overly fussy with their hotel accommodations. We have come to see China, not to inspect its hotel facilities. Despite minor maintenance matters, the facilities in which we stayed were quite adequate.

December 6. Notes on Birth Control

Any number of married persons we met during our trip were surprised not only by the fact that we were traveling with our five children, but also that we should have that many offspring. They proudly proclaimed that they have one or perhaps two. Although the norm was two several years ago, the new ideal in China is "One Child for One Family." This policy of "One Is Best" is being widely trumpeted in view of China's population explosion. Already this growth has put pressure on the severe housing shortage in the cities, as well as on schools and job opportunities. Since only about ten percent of the land can be cultivated, food resources have always been a problem, given the whims of climate. Hence population control is essential.

Since Liberation in 1949, the population has grown from 540 million to an estimated one billion. The goal is to move to zero population growth by the year 2000 and to stabilize the population at about 1.3 billion. All sorts of incentive programs are being mounted. Preferential treatment is given one-child families in applying for schools or jobs. Bonuses, rewards, and inducements are given to parents with smaller families. These rewards include an annual 40-yuan bonus for one-child families, first choice of new housing facilities, and priority entrance to schools and for jobs.

Birth control, sterilization, and abortion programs are widely promoted. All these measures constitute a considerable shift for a country that has traditionally favored large families as a sign of good fortune. Birth control is further complicated, especially in rural areas, by parents who have female progeny and keep trying until a male offspring is produced. Morever, the aggressive new policy goes against an earlier Maoist belief that more people meant more production. Nowadays Chairman Mao's teaching is that "mankind should control its birth rate." Again virtue is the mother of necessity for the world's most populous country!

XI

Return to Guangzhou (Canton)

December 7. Visit to Ancestral Village

Our flight from Guilin returned us to Guangzhou, where our initial journey began, the place our ancestors called home. Being in this city set our family to musing: what if our ancestors had never pulled up stakes and left for America—the land of the "Golden Mountain" ("Jing Shan")? What would our lives be like living here? Even though the time was short, we decided to hire a car to take us to May's family's village, which is about 30 miles away in the countryside. Since my family's village is about 250 miles away, time was simply not available for that foray.

Our visit was a total surprise. When we arrived, the relatives were out working in the fields. One of the cousins hopped on his bicycle and raced away to round up the kinfolks. In a short time about thirty-five people gathered, over half of them small children. We left gifts of candy and cookies, and then my daughters Mellanie, Wendy and Miko offered to take polaroid pictures and give them to each person. This created a flurry of excitement, as the recipients delightfully posed for photos with glee and gaiety.

Work on this agricultural commune is arduous. We did not see any modern machinery in sight. Both the conditions and the farming tools seem rather primitive. The relatives apologized for the untidiness of the place and immediately ushered us outside to the dirt courtyard for tea and conversation. I wondered to myself if this were a typical small village and what I would do to reorganize the conditions so that life would be less rigorous here.

A picture of my deceased father-in-law and his wife was brought out. We chatted about family members living and dead, and the relatives recited the names of my wife's four brothers. We were all escorted to the large, white house, which May's father had sent money to build before the war. Even though the house had seen better days—the Japanese had

ripped off all its metal parts—it looked like a palace compared to the
other living quarters.

Our visit to this rural village brought us all closer to our roots. We
looked at the fertile fields and at the sturdy relatives who seemed to be
unafraid of hard, manual labor. My mind drifted back, and I could well
imagine four generations earlier, when my own great-grandfather emi-
grated to America in order to escape the rigors and privations of a devastating drought and famine that struck the Guangzhou region.

As I cast my eyes about, I could detect residual signs of battles and
bombings from both the war with Japan and the civil war between the
Nationalists and the Communists. Through the decades this village has
endured the ravages of conflict. These are long-suffering people who
lead simple lives. They remain hopeful that their children's generation
will fare better.

We have seen much progress and development in our visits to ten
major cities and some smaller villages in China. However, this visit with
May's relatives is a stark reminder that China is still a poor country and
that the road to modernization has barely begun for many small villages.

Notes on Clothing Style and Colors

As our journey is on its last leg, the reflections come tumbling in cascad-
ing fashion. And so, unable to sleep at three a.m., I search for pen and
paper to capture the fallout.

People in China generally dress in such identical, unisex clothing style
and color that it appears as if everyone is wearing a common uniform
which comes in three rather drab colors—navy blue, army green, and
dark gray.

There are several explanations for the sameness of attire. First, the
style and colors are what is available in the local stores for consumption.
The supply is mass produced for simple and functional use. A second
explanation is that people do not dress in loud, outlandish colors because
they would then stand out in a crowd. Foreigners, like ourselves, draw
undue attention simply by virtue of our curious mode of dress and our
shocking profusion of colors. It just would be inappropriate for elderly
persons to dress in loud colors. By the same token, babies and young
children are expected to wear the bright colors.

Note that one advantage China has in the sameness of attire is the non-
competitive sense of equality that is fostered. In the West, we tend to
measure people by their clothing. Think of how much silly attention,
ridiculous extravagance, and conspicuous display we give to stylish fashions. Our conventions go to the opposite extreme of keeping up with the
latest "in" fads or of calling attention to ourselves through our distinc-
tive styles and colors. When it comes to clothes, I prefer to relax with
whatever is comfortable, rather than be a slave to the struggle to out-
dress the next guy!

Nowadays, one may observe some teenagers and young adults breaking out in varied colors and styles in the streets of China's large cities. Also, young men are allowing their hair to grow longer, and young women are experimenting with different hair styles. These changes are likely to pick up momentum, as contact with Western visitors continues to mount.

On the other hand, peer pressure for conformity is pretty strong and could overwhelm these innovative patterns just now emerging. What changes, and how rapidly they will be adopted, only time will tell. My guess, however, is that ten years from now, foreign journalists will no longer be writing about the drab and dull colors and clothing styles.

My confidence on the side of change in fashions is supported by Beijing's appointment of Hanae Mori and Pierre Cardin to serve as fashion consultants. Already their fashion shows in Shanghai and Beijing have attracted widespread attention. After you've seen Mori and Cardin, can plain and simple clothing styles persist for long?

December 8. More Notes on Democracy Wall

The day after visiting the small village of May's relatives, I heard that action had been taken to scrape off and scrub clean Beijing's Democracy Wall. Thus the year-long experiment came to an official halt. However, I felt a bit better in learning that another locale had been earmarked for wall posters. The new wall is at the picturesque 16th-century "Moon Altar Park," two miles to the west, where emperors once made animal sacrifices to the moon. Here authors must register their names and addresses before posting their dissent. After registration, the poster is to be hung without prior inspection by the officials. First reports indicate that the new wall, though located in a less populous area, is as popular as its predecessor.

Why the change? From what I can gather, the Party leadership is said to be concerned about political stability and national unity in this time of transition when the idea is to focus on the goals of modernization. Registration is to ensure that writers are held accountable for libel or to refrain from making reckless charges. I suppose that there is some legitimacy for these concerns, given the existence of a network of minority dissent and the recency of the Gang of Four. Who knows? They may still have supporters.

Democracy Wall also is said to have created an "image" problem. It did receive an inordinate amount of attention of the foreign correspondents stationed in Beijing. Journalists everywhere tend to pounce on negative news more avidly. Such headline-provoking, sensational stories in the foreign press appeared offensive to the leadership, which is unaccustomed to hanging out its dirty linen anyway.

My hope is that the new, "regulated" Democracy Wall will continue to serve a useful purpose. Although I personally would affirm the institution of Democracy Wall, I am also mindful of the fact that gigantic strides have been made in eliminating other walls—the walls that prevented contact with Western nations for decades, the walls of isolation, of censorship in the theater and the arts, the walls that closed down temples, churches, and mosques, and the walls that foster hunger, poverty, illiteracy, and ill health. These walls have come tumbling down in the past few years. Their destruction, in my opinion, is a tremendous source of hope.

Still More Notes on the Cultural Revolution

In various cities that we visited, invariably we would strike up conversations with local residents. Often someone would overhear us speaking in English and approach us to comment that he or she could speak the language or had studied in America thirty-five or forty years ago. They are just as eager to know what's happened in San Francisco, Evanston, Ithaca, or New York City during the intervening years as we are to pick their brains on what's happening in China.

Sooner or later, after we have established rapport, the subject of the Cultural Revolution surfaces for discussion. A few persons we met were reluctant to say anything, except that they had suffered indignities which were obviously still painful. However, many others spoke freely about their experiences. Earlier in this journal I remarked on the devastating impact of the Cultural Revolution. Here I wish to present three vignettes of particular persons—what they were doing and how they felt about this critical period.

1. One man in his mid-thirties, now employed as a writer, told us that he was a member of the Red Guard. He had just finished two years at the university. As a student leader, he responded to the call to become politically active and quit studying. With a group of friends who had musical and dramatic talents, he roamed around the country, traveling by railway without paying any fares, going to different cities and campuses, where his group put on revolutionary performances and conducted rallies.

He personally witnessed other Red Guard members giving short haircuts to people with long hair, destroying property gathered from the temples, burning books on campuses, and holding "court trials" of professors. However, he claims he himself never took part in these more militant activities. Nor was he a party to any of the pitched battles between rival Red Guard factions, although he witnessed some fierce and savage fighting which led to killings on campuses he visited. His dramas and speeches emphasized ridding China of the influence of foreign culture and ridiculed the ancient traditions, which were branded as "feudal" or "Confucian."

Why did he do these things? He claimed that he participated in these activities because it was the patriotic thing to be doing at the time; it was a way for young people to become involved in politics and to help out their country against the "capitalist roaders." Besides, it was fun to be traveling around with his friends.

Now he realizes that it was a mistake. Despite only finishing two years of higher education, he and others like him were granted their university diplomas. He doesn't feel terribly good about this, for he realizes that opportunities for learning were lost and that he is not fully qualified academically. At the time, he thought he could do no less, since he sought to serve his country as a loyal member of the Party and of the Red Guard.

2. A university professor gave us some very perceptive insights. He was quite adamant in pointing out that to call it a Cultural Revolution is a misnomer. If anything, the movement set culture behind at least a decade, if not longer. He claimed it was a cultural regression. It side-tracked the modernization movement, which was already well under way up to 1966.

This American-trained professor insisted that instead of being a Cultural Revolution it was really a political movement, a test of political enthusiasm and "correct" political thinking that was being demanded. In the beginning, this political thrust was intended to be a corrective to save the country from going down the capitalistic road. But soon afterwards, the movement got deflected to serve the private gain of amassing political power. A political network was formed and coalitions were made with petty politicians at provincial and local levels—which the professor likened to the Tammany Hall crowd in New York City or the Mayor Daley machine in Chicago.

The Gang of Four capitalized upon this political turmoil to seize power in a subversive manner. They took over control of the newspapers and other organs of communication, under the guise of patriotism. They whipped up an atmosphere of hysteria, which brought the nation to an economic standstill. Industrial output lagged, unemployment was high, and both workers and students were wandering around.

When I asked how a small group of people could possibly gain so much power, he called my attention to the French Revolution. When the monarchy was initially overthrown, a chaotic form of democracy was instituted. Then followed the wild and hysterical days of torture chambers, cruel punishments, riots in Paris, beheading of Louis XVI, Marie Antoinette, and even Robespierre, and the inquisitions.* When the French Revolution got out of hand, inflation skyrocketed, production came to a halt, and unemployment soared. Then the professor brought up the subject of the Salem witchcraft in which an entire community could become irrational. These things happen in history, he mused.

This well-informed and learned professor (I began to wonder who had drawn the "bamboo curtain"—they or we) went on to caution about the use of power when it is in the hands of the few, who serve their own self-interest rather than serving the common welfare. What started out as a reforming or cleansing movement ended up as a power grab to serve selfish, private interests for power.

Now I could understand the attack on traditional values as a contest for loyalty; I could even see the perverse logic of attacking temples and

---

*Indeed, in China too the Revolution ultimately destroyed its Robespierre—defense minister and Mao's heir apparent Lin Biao.

churches and foreign things. But what strikes me as hard to comprehend, I told the professor, was why the Gang of Four would want to disrupt industrial production by calling on workers to strike. That just seems to hurt people's livelihood and the nation's economic well-being. He answered: It was a ploy to discredit the extant leadership, to bring the economy to collapse so they could step in and assume power. Wow! Now I see.

How was the professor personally affected by the Cultural Revolution? Deeply—in no small part, due to his previous academic training in America and his fluency with American scientific literature and research methods. His university, where he serves as a senior professor ("the more senior, the more vulnerable," he mused), was shut down for three years. The Cultural Revolution began in 1966. By 1968, it hit his campus with a vengeance. Another class of students was not to be admitted until 1970. During the entire period of the Cultural Revolution, an active campaign was waged against the value of learning. Students were told to take to the streets and engage in political activities. We had much to share in discussions about the student unrest and a similar mentality that held sway among American students in the 1960s. We also commented on student strikes in Paris, in Tokyo, and in Korea. In China, education was paralyzed not only in the colleges but also in the high schools and even in the primary schools. Graduates of high schools were admonished not to enroll for colleges, but to go directly to the rural areas and learn about agriculture.

The professor himself was ordered to recant, to repent for his foolish and wrong thoughts and undesirable way of living. He was "examined" publicly and had to write out his wrongdoings in an essay and also acknowledge that he was a bad influence among the students. This was a bitter pill to swallow, for he obviously loved teaching and is a very effective communicator. He had to acknowledge that his past training and present thoughts were not suitable for China. He said rather sadly that he did all these things under duress, but in his own mind he could conscientiously admit that his training and teachings were not appropriate for the China *of that particular time.* He noted that other colleagues fared less well and were shipped off to farming communes to do menial labor or were purposely given such jobs as cleaning out the latrines.

With the demise of the Gang of Four, the nightmare ended. He and many of his colleagues were reinstated. Order and stability were restored. The professor is very optimistic about China's future. He thinks that the great majority of the people—peasants along with intellectuals—realize that modernization or rebuilding and reconstructing China is necessary. "Without it, our people cannot survive economically or politically," were his closing remarks.

I was deeply moved by this encounter. I appreciated not only his insights, but his candor and openness. At no time did I sense any fear or hesitation to share his thoughts and feelings in response to my queries. We met as strangers and parted as friends.

3. A young woman, who now works as an English language interpreter, was willing to share her experiences. She first caught my attention because her very attractive, delicate face seemed incongruous with her rough-appearing hands, which looked as if they were accustomed to hard labor. When the Cultural Revolution started in 1966, she was only ten years old. Her father was manager of a large factory. At home she never had to do any work.

At the beginning, she simply tagged along with members of the Red Guard as they moved about the city. She became part of the crowd that participated in rallies and political teach-ins. After graduating from middle school, instead of going directly to high school, she heeded the call for volunteers to go into the countryside. She referred to this practice as "ideological remolding,"* wherein young urban youth set an example by committing themselves to hard labor in rural communes. This meant volunteering to take on the most difficult tasks in order to fulfill the goals and help the socialist cause.

For three years, from the age of fifteen to eighteen, she joined a poor agricultural commune and learned to respect the ways of peasants. She worked in the fields planting rice and wheat. In view of her background, the work at first was hard and heavy. However, she actually enjoyed her time spent with the peasants. She found them considerate and understanding and grateful for the help of the young people from the cities.

Even without a high-school education, she volunteered to go to Beijing University in 1974. She passed an entrance examination and was nominated by her commune to study at the university. In 1978, she received her degree, majoring in English language. All her expenses at the university were paid by the state.

On the whole, she claimed her experience was a good one. She regarded the Cultural Revolution as a good thing that had beneficial results. These are her reasons:

1. It was launched by our great leader, Chairman Mao Zedong.

2. It got rid of many superstitions that had been hanging on tenaciously, such as Taoism and ancestor worship. For example, when people in the villages were sick, they would often go to the temple to pray and burn incense, instead of going to the doctor. They believed that God could solve all their problems. Another example is in family and marriage. Prior to the Cultural Revolution, many marriages were arranged by parents, so that the groom did not see his bride until the wedding ceremony. Nowadays, many marriages are by the free choice of the young people who decide for themselves.

3. The position of men and women is more equal since the Cultural Revolution.˙

---

*I could not really figure out whether she meant to say "remodeling" (the word she spelled out for me), or "remolding"—a common Maoist expression pertaining to the reshaping of thoughts at the May 4th Schools established by Mao's directive of May 7th, 1966. These schools taught others to learn from the peasants, to work with their hands in the fields, to cleanse their thoughts.

4. Another good practice is to send educated people and doctors to work with the minority nationalities in the remote, autonomous regions, such as Tibet, Inner Mongolia, and Xinjiang.

I commented to the young interpreter that I was glad she brought out these beneficial aspects of the Cultural Revolution. She quickly replied that there were also negative consequences and began reciting these:

1. Lin Biao and the Gang of Four did damage to the Cultural Revolution by changing the policies that had been decided by the Central Committee of the Party.

2. The Gang of Four took over the Cultural Revolution. They were very clever in contriving slogans.

3. The Cultural Revolution limited the development of science and technology.

4. Factory workers were discouraged from producing and were asked to slow down production. They were told that increased productivity would only help the "revisionist capitalist roaders."

5. The Cultural Revolution put pressure on intellectuals, scientists, and older revolutionaries, who were veterans of the War of Liberation. It claimed that they were bad elements and urged that they be gotten rid of.

According to my thoughtful informant, the young people are really not to be blamed. They were just following their leaders and many joined as a result of peer pressure. They were inexperienced and thought they were being loyal and helpful. But actually, she said, a lot of harm was done in damaging properties—especially historic relics and stone inscriptions. In her experience, the worst period of destruction was from lage 1965 to 1968, although other parts of the country may have started later.

How does she feel now? Looking back, she says she would not have joined in the activities of the Red Guard. She claims she has learned to be more critical, to analyze a situation, think for herself, and not just follow along slavishly. However, she does not regret the time spent in the countryside, working with the peasants.

Here again is an impressive young woman—committed, idealistic, articulate and willing to work hard, to play her role in ensuring that China will be a new nation. She too has much faith and confidence in the goals of modernization.

Notes on Significant Events of Mythic Power

Every society can point to those epoch-making, evocative moments that seem to have mythic power and appeal. They serve to unite and congeal the energies of a people. They are rallying points which galvanize highly charged emotions. Thus we in America refer to Gettysburg, Selma, or Woodstock.

For a nation whose regime is only thirty years young, whose leaders have sought to transform values that have persisted for thousands of years, I believe the significant events of mythic power are: the Long March, Liberation, the Cultural Revolution, and the Modernization movement.

1. *The Long March* is of such decisive and heroic character that it will always be associated with struggle and survival, and the sheer determination to overcome seemingly insurmountable odds. It is possible to dare to think the unthinkable, to do the impossible. Those who took part in the ordeal of the Long March share a close communion, a mystical spirit of camaraderie, that others may only seek to emulate or to share in vicariously. The power of the image in present-day affairs is attested to by the numerous references to the "New Long March" when summoning the people to current goals, quotas, and achievements in various endeavors of life and work.

2. *Liberation* is to be set free from the humiliation, bondages and oppressions of the past (whether from foreigners or aristocrats, warlords or landlords), and to build a new egalitarian society. Above all, "Liberation" refers to the founding of the People's Republic of China on October 1, 1949. Nearly everyplace we visited, whether it be factory, school or commune, constant comparative references were made to the conditions that prevailed before Liberation and the new situation following Liberation. I have grown so accustomed to this bifurcation in historical time that it seems appropriate to coin the designation "B.L." (Before Liberation) and "A.L." (After Liberation). To the Chinese, it seems as significant as our B.C. and A.D. Of course, 1949 marks the year A.L. To pick just two comparative examples: B.L., foreign scholars had concluded that China's continental sedimentation contained no oil. A.L., Chinese geologists located many rich deposits. China began its own program of exploration, drilling, extraction, refining, and petrochemical technology. B.L. saw China caught up in soaring and staggering inflation rates. What had cost one yuan in 1937 inflated to 8,500 million yuan on the eve of Liberation! A.L. stabilized the economy and put a halt to inflation, which has been almost negligible for thirty years. Despite fits and starts, economic development was under way after Liberation.

3. A third great symbol of modern China, which brought the nation to the brink of political and economic collapse, is the *Cultural Revolution* and the Gang of Four. The tumult and turmoil of this period has left an incalculable imprint. Even now the nation has not yet fully recovered from the shock waves of the Cultural Revolution. Until the public trial of the Gang of Four is finished and becomes history, anxieties, bordering on fear, a wait-and-see attitude, will still grip the minds of some. Many people regard the decade of prominence of the Cultural Revolution as an aberration, a period of interruption, a cultural regression that has now been exorcised from the body politic. Both the gains and the losses of this period are bound to leave their marks on the consciousness of the Chinese people.

4. *The Modernization Movement*—referred to as the "New Long March"—has designated four fields of advancement: agriculture, indus-

try, national defense, and science/technology. A target date has been set for the year 2000. Many of the signs and slogans seen throughout China today pertain to Modernization. The push is on to accelerate Modernization, even if it means modifying the principle of self-reliance and seeking joint ventures with foreign nations.

I personally believe it would be difficult for China to pull off an "operation bootstraps." Besides, there is no need to reinvent the wheel. In our shrunken planet that is now spaceship earth, no nation can go it alone. Every nation is interdependent. China needs our scientific technology today. Some day we may have to rely upon China's rich, untapped store of oil!

I, for one, would not want to underestimate the potentialities of a people who have a record of getting things done—whether it be the Great Wall in the past or the underground cities of the present. Unless the modernization goals are derailed by another effort at imposing ideological purity, political rectitude over developmental goals, present-day China is at the take-off stage. It is poised for fundamental changes, which will determine the future course of its national destiny. With its vast mineral and fossil-fuel resources yet unused, I believe that China will welcome the year 2000 as a modern, industrial power.

December 8. Farewell to China

Several members of our travel group have decided to stay over in Guangzhou for four or five extra days in order to visit with their relatives in the villages. These unplanned, special trips reminded us that China Travel Service was most obliging in making arrangements for us to go wherever we wished off the beaten path. One should not carry the older belief that visitors to China see only what the authorities want them to see. That simply is untrue. Note that books published by China travelers just a few years ago claimed that visitors were prevented from having direct personal contact with ordinary Chinese people, that frank discussions were impossible, and all contacts were pre-arranged. In our experience, this situation has completely changed and renders earlier observations obsolete. We encountered no difficulties or restrictions. We walked, talked, and visited at our pleasure.

Since we had accumulated so many worldly possessions in our "buy, buy, buy" mania, and were literally bulging at the seams, we took this opportunity to lighten our load. Our family gathered nearly all of our clothing and extra shoes for our friends to take to the people in the villages.

After repacking our gear, it was time for a farewell party with our China Travel Service guide. His name is Nep. Very early we nicknamed him "Nipper." Young, strong, and goodlooking, Nipper's rapport with the group grew steadily, until, at the end, parting was full of sorrow. He had become a member of the family. He spoke only Mandarin and Cantonese, and was assigned to our group because of the paucity of English-speaking guides, given the sudden demand. One of the few words of English he spoke was "Come on—let's go" in a slow drawl, which we constantly imitated.

Since our children spoke no Chinese and Nipper spoke virtually no English, one interesting development was that our children and Nipper taught each other. Nipper learned many English words and phrases, while our children began to speak and understand many Chinese words as the trip progressed. Promises were exchanged that the next time we meet, Nipper would be speaking English and we Mandarin.

The party was held in Nipper's room. We all crowded into his small quarters, sang songs, and toasted one another with "Gum Beis" (Bottoms Up). It was a gala, festive, joyous occasion, appropriate for a family parting. We presented gifts to Nipper (another "no-no" myth to be discarded) who responded with effusive words of appreciation in English and yet another, final song in Chinese. His English sentences were bolder now. It tugged at our hearts when he said, "I will miss you."

Parting was difficult, for saying goodbye to Nipper also meant saying farewell to China. He had been our guide and our friend. We will miss him too, as we will miss China. For our family, the People's Republic of China is no longer an unknown, remote or mysterious place. Instead, our experience of China is a warm, hospitable and spirited nation, throbbing with vitality, rushing toward modernization, and eager to welcome visitors to share its aspirations. However, in all our exhilaration and weariness, it felt good to be homeward bound.

December 9. Hong Kong Culture Shock

Before heading straight home to California, we decided to spend a few days in the British Crown Colony of Hong Kong. What a culture shock! It felt like moving from the gentle breezes to the whirlwind. Or like coming out of the dark caves to the still dimly lit world of Guilin, and then suddenly confront the bright, dazzling, brash neon lights of Hong Kong.

As I stepped onto the platform at the train station in Hong Kong, I immediately felt swept up in a hurly-burly, hectic pace of life. In fact, once when I slowed down from my double-time cadence, an older, wiry woman, carrying two immense packages suspended from a bamboo pole on her shoulders, whacked me on the backside and nearly sent me careening off the platform onto the train tracks!

Dodging bicycles with their constant, musical ting-a-lings in China is one matter. But once we hit the streets of Hong Kong, avoiding onrushing cars, cabs and trucks, which are no respecters of persons, is quite another matter. Truly I felt like someone from another planet. Here there are only the quick and the dead.

When our bus brought us to the ultramodern Miramar Hotel in Kowloon, I stepped into a lobby lit by thousands of lightbulbs, which were made even brighter by reflecting off mirrored ceilings, which in turn caught the lush, maroon carpeting below. What an incredibly garish sight—a cross between Caesar's Palace and Circus Circus in Las Vegas. At first I blinked. Then I squinted. Then I got accustomed to the glare. At least Hong Kong is spared from the energy crisis!

Many people are dressed in Hong Kong as if they just stepped out of the photos of the latest fashion magazines. I began staring at all these fashion plates, dressed as I was in my only remaining rags. Now I can understand why people stared at us in China. Platform shoes, straight-leg and flared pants, three-piece knit suits were everywhere in sight. Women wearing heavy make-up, perfumed to the hilt, and sporting the latest hair styles naturally caught my attention in contrast to the natural, simple look of faces we grew accustomed to in China.

In an effort to stop my head from spinning, I went out for a walk around the hotel and around Nathan Road. My immediate impressions: Hong Kong is one vast supermarket. Everyone is on the make. It is free enterprise run rampant. Cowboy capitalism rides again. Anything and everything may be had at a price. Fine jewelry and expensive Swiss watches, precious diamonds and jade, stereos and pocket computers from Japan, rugs from India or the Middle East. I lost count of the number of stores I passed by which sold nude and lewd magazines, which would be inconceivable in China. Finally, as I ambled along in my half-dazed manner, a young man stopped me to ask if I "wanted a nice Hong Kong girl for the night!"

It was time to head back to the hotel. Suddenly I felt a tingle of nervousness that it was not altogether safe and sound for me to be meandering by myself at night in the streets of Hong Kong, and I quickened my pace. I never had this feeling of apprehension in China, despite the early morning or late night hours during which we walked the streets.

I cannot help contrasting all these impressions and feelings that come to mind with the past month's experiences in China, where nearly the opposite picture holds true. A tale of two cities? Is this what is in store for China with the achievement of modernization? God forbid! Would that it were possible to take the best and discard the worst features, to separate the wheat from the chaff in developing societies.

The next day or so I gradually become reoriented to the ways of the West. Or perhaps I should say I am getting re-occidized. Now that my culture shock is wearing off, I know it is unfair to compare cultures—though we all do it involuntarily, if not ethnocentrically. It is even more unfair to compare the worst features of one culture with the best of another. I know I could survive in the world that is Hong Kong, for I have mastered some of the arts of stepping lively in a competitive, acquisitive, individualistic climate. As one of my colleagues is fond of saying of himself, "I have a highly developed sense of self-preservation."

Whether I could survive in the cultural ethos of China, given its different socio-economic-political context, is quite another matter. In short, China is a marvelous place to visit, a vast stretching and learning experience, which fills our family with a sense of awe and pride for China's achievements in the past and the present, but I am not sure I could live there. All the more reason to look foward to coming home!

*
* *

EPILOGUE A

Notes on Future Trends and Problem Areas

The image of the stable may be appropriate for a horse-and-buggy age. In recent decades, however, turbulence has supplanted stability as the sign of the times.

To say that present-day China is experiencing a period of transition seems like a platitude or a pedestrian observation—almost like claiming that babies have mothers. This contention sounds all the more commonplace because not only China, but the entire world is caught up in a process of transformation. "The future ain't what it used to be" anywhere in the world—certainly not in the Middle East (Iran), in Central Asia (Afghanistan), in Southeast Asia (Cambodia), in Africa (Ghana, Uganda), in Latin America or in the U.S. The past two decades have been filled with turmoil.

It is quite likely that as we face the challenges of the 1980s, the world will change more rapidly than we are able to change ourselves. Yet the flat truth is that for China one period known as the Cultural Revolution has ended, and another era known as the Modernization Movement has been initiated. What was once acceptable has now been repudiated. What will be is not all that clear, except that the march to modernization is on the way.

For the past century and a half, none of the transitions in China has been smooth. Indeed, Chairman Mao was fond of saying that "a revolution is not an invitation to a dinner party." The road to modernization will be paved with potholes and detours too. What some of these pitfalls will be is surely open for conjecture. My own personal assessment would include the following prospects and problem areas:

1. *Economic Development.* What kind of economy is emerging? My guess is that more and more we will see a "mixed" economy. One would have to be blind to ignore the improvements in the Chinese economy since Liberation. People are not starving and dying in the streets. Children are no longer diseased and infected with rickets. China is no longer the "sick man of Asia." Hundreds of thousands of beggars do not line the streets. School, health, and sanitation systems have improved. Although poverty and famine are eliminated, China is still a poor country. Many

places, especially villages in rural areas, are still backward. The push is on for modernization, which is the wave of the future, for a wholesale improvement of China's economic well-being. What that wave will drown out in the way of ancient or present-day values remains to be seen. More recent emphases upon personal incentives, bonuses, individual recognition for achievement, private plots for cultivation, sales at the "free" market for personal gain, acknowledgment of profit as a valid criterion of industrial performance, as well as massive foreign investments in joint venture technological projects (new airports and offshore oil explorations)—all these developments are moving the Chinese economy, I think, toward a "mixed" economy and away from the more rigid Maoist policies of a decade ago. Who knows? Perhaps the dialectics of history call for the U.S. to move more toward a planned economy (with our Penn Central and Chrysler bailouts) and China to go in the direction of a "mixed" economy. If the past is any predictor, however, there is bound to be turbulence in these transitions.

2. *Political Stability.* The degree of political stability in the future seems to me to be a crucial problem. A history of fits and starts and lurches, first in this direction and then in the opposite, is very detrimental and demoralizing—except for those who covet perpetual revolution as a way of life. But that's no way to run a railroad or a country. Leaders who found themselves in favor one year would suddenly fall out of favor and be denounced the next year. Ideas that were discredited one year and their proponents purged become warmly embraced a few years later. Ironically, personal success can bring disfavor and downfall. The resulting turmoil, the oscillations and vacillations, have created uncertainty and immobility and even encouraged cynicism. Doubtless, the Cultural Revolution was a period for unleashing of passions, turbulence and even violence. The question remains whether such *luan* (confusion) will be episodic or chronic. So long as this condition of political instability persists, significant strides toward modernization will elude the Chinese people. My guess is that the future is likely to see more openness in many spheres of life and at the same time periodic pull-backs or even clamping down on tendencies that have gone too far too fast. With an aging leadership and the demise of the charismatic revolutionary veterans, the problem of political stability is likely to continue to plague China. What form and shape "democratic centralism" will assume will bear watching. What will be the nature of the balance between the left leg of "revolution and equality" and the right leg of "modernization and merit"? Whether a political or a pragmatic test will be applied will be of interest. An agricultural commune we visited used to meet for political indoctrination two nights a week. When I inquired why these meetings have been discarded, the leader's response was: "Now we work more and talk less!" Will this spirit of pragmatism prevail?

3. *The Russians Are Coming!* One of the ironies of history is sure to be the changeover from friend to foe that marks the relationship between these two Communist powers. Some would argue that the mutual enmity

and suspicion is not a product of recent decades but dates way back into earlier centuries before the modern era. In Chinese history, it seems as if the "enemy" is always coming from the north. Apart from their international rivalry in the Communist world, there is the territorial dispute over 1.5 million square miles that the Chinese claim the czars grabbed under unequal treaties and unfair duress. The Russians deny this claim categorically. Call it xenophobia if you like, but from our experience in China the fear of the Russians is a real thing. Having tasted the sting of foreign oppression, China refuses to buckle under or be subjugated to Russia. China keeps a wary eye on the massive military build-up of over a million troops on the Russian side of its extensive 5,000-mile northern border, which the the two nations share. Since 1969, sporadic border fighting has erupted, angry confrontations have not subsided, and the Sino-Soviet Commission seems incapable of resolving differences, or even agreeing upon an agenda. And now the incursion into Afghanistan makes military bedfellows out of China and the United States! *They* are saying that at long last *we* are beginning to recognize the dangers of "hegemonism." Now America and China enter the era of the "eagle-dragon embrace." The People's Liberation Army is familiar with encirclement strategies, so it will be on guard to see if this is, indeed, Russia's design. We have seen the underground cities, and the supposition is that they are in readiness for a Russian nuclear attack. One well-versed professor with whom we spoke was convinced that it was to Russia's advantage to attack pre-emptively sooner rather than later, when China's navy and air force will have improved and its nuclear weaponry system, far behind Russia's, will have made significant strides. All this talk of a preventive first strike by Russia to neutralize China prior to economic and military gains being made by the Chinese is, I must confess, surprising and sobering to hear. But we cannot deny it as a real feeling that we encountered. In fact, one person said it was not a question of whether but *when* China and Russia will do battle! I have no way of knowing how bitter the rivalry is or whether the Sino-Soviet split will lead to open conflict or reconciliation, but I can only hope for the sake of global survival that things are not as bad as they seem to be.

4. *Middle Management Bureaucracy.* Obviously a managed country needs many managers. We are familiar with political candidates in our country vowing to cut down on the bureaucracy under government payroll, only to leave office with more agencies and bureaucrats than ever before. We have previously alluded to the problem of middle management immobility and inertia. We can only earmark this as a critical problem for the future, not only because momentum is arrested in achieving national goals, but also because this is the source of a new elitism based on privilege and power. Many are the protests, cynical jokes, and grievances of the common people against the middle management bureaucrats. I don't know how to resolve this situation short of political stability, a sense of confidence, and early retirements.

5. *Urban and Rural Tensions.* We have already seen gaps and discrep-

ancies in income and life style between rural and urban dwellers. The poorest areas seem to be in remote villages away from the cities. Mao sensed the deprivations of the peasants in starting his revolutionary movement in the countryside. Yet ironically the people in the rural areas do not seem to have derived as many benefits as have the urban dwellers. With an 80% rural and 20% urban population spread, this seems to me to be too lopsided a proportion. Recall that in the U.S. such a proportion of rural/urban population was true of the early 1800s. Then a relentless shift to urbanization took place until by 1900 the nation was 64% rural, while nowadays the figure has dropped to about 30%. Since China's policy has been to hold down urban growth, I doubtless will be criticized for this proposal, but I can't help thinking that China's standard of living will be increased by quantum leaps with increased urbanization of the country. Eventually it will take fewer people to grow the crops to feed the population. New industries will blossom in cities and their environs and will take up the population slack. To bridge the gap between rural and urban differences, a "rurban" policy of satellite towns that combine both rural and urban advantages might well be mounted. I have read or heard no discussion of this, but my proposal would be to work toward a 60% rural and 40% urban population distribution. Already we have seen young people by the droves moving back to urban areas and creating problems associated with dislocation. I think the population shift will continue to go from rural to urban areas. After all, when you've been to Paris, how can you go back to the farm? The same may be said of Shanghai or Beijing. So I see a better urban/rural balance in China's future.

6. *Population Stability.* With improved public health and medical care, life is preserved at the beginning and prolonged at the end to create even more population pressures for the most populous nation on the globe. If the theories of the Reverend Thomas Malthus are applicable, China surely provides the soil for testing. Continuing population increase would be bound to absorb economic gains and retard higher standards of living. Unless productivity is maximized, as envisioned in the march to Modernization, population growth will in due time outstrip available resources. Stringent measures are now being adopted to check runaway growth which would threaten the Modernization goals. How successful these measures will be it is too early to tell. So far the evidence seems to be contradictory. I think that important strides are being made, although to some the measures may seem harsh. I trust that China has not awakened too late to the population bomb.* Doubtless the campaign to curtail population growth will be stepped up. Just a short time ago, the ideal was set forth as two children. Now that has been shifted to only

---

* In an article on "New Population Theory," written by the then president of Beijing University in 1957, when China's population as 656 million, Dr. Ma Yinchu warned about unchecked population growth and its disadvantageous impact on the standard of living. He was severely criticized and forced to resign from his post, and further research on population problems was stymied. His views turned out to be correct after all.

one. We can attest that children are much loved in China. So holding the line will take a special kind of discipline. Population control and stability will remain a pressing problem for China.

7. *Erosion of Unity and Discipline.* This is a difficult and amorphous issue to tackle. We kept hearing that in the early years of Liberation, there was unity and discipline, a kind of cohesiveness and esprit that seems to be lacking these days. Another way of expressing it is the dedication to the work spirit, the tenacity of purpose, a sense of self-sacrifice that made China appear to be a very moral society. In the early days, some observers even referred to the New China as a "Puritan society." Those who cast aspersions called it a "regimented" or "repressed" society. But others saw a discipline and commonality of purpose and mission, something to be admired—given the laxity, aimlessness, and solipsistic hedonism prevailing in the West. Of course, historically speaking, the problem of political unity and national cohesiveness has plagued China from time immemorial. China has more often been fragmented than united. Moreover, there is the problem of the dialectic between freedom on the one hand, and discipline or order on the other. A correlation that says the more freedom the less discipline seems at least plausible.

A persisting question will be the future of the group ethic—that spirit of working together, of serving the people, and uniting in concert to achieve national goals; for it was precisely this highly developed consciousness of common purpose, unity, and discipline that has enabled China to come this far.

If we take at face value the laments we heard about the erosion of unity and discipline—bearing in mind the recent chaotic decade of the Cultural Revolution—then it appears that China's future must entail a recovery of purpose, social discipline, or vision. There is a playing down of anything that resembles a personality cult in these post-Mao days. Chairman Hua is not featured in the same sense that Mao was. He who calls the tune, Vice Premier Deng, is certainly a behind-the-scenes operator. What or where, then, is the source of a new vision likely to emanate from?

I personally have high hopes for the charisma of an idea—and not the fragile, fickle charisma revolving around a person. My hope is that China will cut out the interpersonal feuding and get on with the task of rebuilding on a firm foundation. That is, to rally around a goal rather than a personality cult may prove sounder and healthier. For the moment, that goal is Modernization.

In many respects, the decade of the 1980s will be a crucial time of testing for the "Great Revolution" that is now thirty years old. Since the thirtieth birthday signifies adulthood and maturity in Chinese culture, this new decade marks the coming of age of China's revolution. A socialist system is now firmly grounded. No longer will it be possible to blame its shortcomings on the Gang of Four and the madness of the Cultural Revolution.

The road ahead is sure to be filled with twists and turns. Nothing has come easily for China during the past century and a half. For that matter, the course of modernization in the West has not been smooth either. We have survived major crises. Were it not for the early dehumanization and brutalization of the Industrial Revolution in the West, one wonders whether a lonely figure named Karl Marx would have had reason to pen his *Manifesto*. Ironically, Marx's response to the ills of "modernization" inspired a revolution to reawaken the world's oldest continuing civilization, which itself is now marching along in pursuit of modernization.

Efforts at modernization in China are bound to be accompanied by turbulence during this period of transition. I am encouraged to believe that one-fourth of the human race, with characteristic hard work, a modicum of stability, and a little bit of luck, will succeed in reaching its goal.

What China does with its power and influence, for good or for ill, once it achieves modernization, whether or not China will reassert its "Middle Kingdom" complex, will be another story for some future chronicler to relate.

*\
* *

EPILOGUE B

Reopening Church Doors in China

By Robert Lee and Frank Mar

What an exciting time to be in China! A new spirit is in the air—a spirit of openness, of "seeking truth from facts." Older ideological slogans have been removed, painted over, or replaced. A shift from ideological rhetoric to "pragmatic realism" is evident.

One of the many signs of the new spirit of openness is that Christian churches are reopening their doors in a number of major cities. Although still in the early stages, one hears about new openings with regularity. This fact should be an occasion for rejoicing. It should also be a call to caution for us in the West, lest well-intentioned, missionary-minded groups repeat past mistakes.

The authors were privileged to join an Overseas Chinese group which visited ten major cities during the month of November and part of December, 1979. Reports by Western journalists that a few churches are resuming public worship services have been filtering back to American readers. Thus far, however, the information has been sketchy and fragmentary.

Although we make no claims for an exhaustive survey, this article hopes to contribute to the growing body of available data about the reopening of churches in China. We have had the advantage of being on the spot and of visiting with two groups of pastors who were involved in reopening congregations in Guangzhou (Canton) and in Hangzhou (Hangchow). We can therefore report their experiences in considerable detail.

Several preliminary points need clarification: First, a number of churches had been closed earlier in 1957, following the period of Chairman Mao's abortive plea to "Let a Hundred Flowers Blossom." Secondly, the well-publicized period of the Cultural Revolution, which can be dated roughly between 1966 and 1976, dealt a devastating blow to churches, temples and mosques. Many of them were destroyed, damaged, or taken over by the Red Guard. Groups of rampaging youth, known as the Red Guard, had free run of the country. They sought to destroy the

This article appeared in the January 23 and 30, 1980, issues of *East/West Chinese American Journal,* and the January 30, 1980, issue of *The Christian Century.*

old traditions as well as shake up the entrenched bureaucracy. They were engaged in closing schools, factories, churches and temples; burning books; destroying ancient writings; and conducting political rallies.

It was during this period of the Cultural Revolution that *public* worship in churches came to a halt. Not only churches, but temples and mosques were similarly affected. Let us cite merely two examples:

In Taiyuan in the Shanxi province, we visited the Tai Ching Tze Buddhist monastery, which dates back to antiquity and has preserved over four thousand ancient texts. It had been closed for ten years between 1967 and 1977. Damage to the temple property is still evident. Before the Cultural Revolution, fifteen hundred to two thousand people were actively associated with the temple, along with forty resident monks. Now about twenty people participate with only four monks, all of whom are elderly. When we asked the Master why there are so few participants, his reasons were two: (1) the people don't know the temple has reopened, and (2) the people are still afraid to take part in view of the previous upheaval they had experienced. The Master noted that one other Buddhist temple has been reactivated in the city. He also knew of five Christian churches that were operating prior to the Cultural Revolution. All were closed down, damaged, or occupied. Although none of the churches has resumed activities, the Master understands that in 1980 they will be resuming services.

In the ancient city of Xi'an (Sian), capital for eleven dynasties, where the tomb of Emperor Qin Shi Huang (221–207 B.C.) is just now being excavated and promises to rival King Tut's in significance, we visited a mosque which serves the minority group known as the Hui people. There we discovered that sixty thousand Hui people live in Xi'an, half of whom are currently associated with the mosque, which has been in continuous existence for thirteen hundred years. Services at the mosque were shut down from 1967 to 1970 by the Cultural Revolution. Nowadays over one thousand adherents engage in religious activities at the mosque every Friday evening. Interestingly enough, the mosque bears no resemblance to traditional Muslim architectural style, but is completely indigenized.

II

Everywhere we traveled, we raised the question about reopened churches. To our pleasant surprise, we were able to compile quite a list. This is particularly noteworthy in view of Tracy K. Jones's claim, stated in July, 1979, that "organized Christianity in the People's Republic of China has, as far as we can see, disappeared" (*Occasional Bulletin of Missionary Research,* July, 1979, p. 90). Jones, who is General Secretary of the United Methodist Board of Global Ministries, repeated this assertion three times in the article. Also, China traveler David Finkelstein, writing an extremely one-sided piece in the *New Yorker* (September 10, 1979, p. 149), quotes a Shanghai native: "No churches have opened in Shanghai. And if they did, it still wouldn't be safe to go."

Apparently five thousand people who attend the Mo-an Church (formerly Moore Memorial) in Shanghai, filling to capacity the facilities in two worship services) do not agree with Finkelstein's informant. In addition, two other Protestant churches, Chin Sin and Hu Pi, have opened their doors to a combined 2,300 worshippers, and the St. Ignatius Roman Catholic Church has resumed mass in November, 1979.

Cities throughout China are reporting reactivated churches. Attendance at public worship services is growing dramatically and will continue to increase. In Beijing, two Protestant churches and the Immaculate Conception Roman Catholic Church conduct services. When we were in Beijing in November, 1979, about 100 attended a Protestant congregation and 50 were at the Roman Catholic mass. By March, 1980, a group of 25 American YMCA national leaders visiting Beijing found themselves worshipping with over 1,000 Chinese in the Roman Catholic mass and 350 in the Protestant Church, which is searching for larger quarters since its present building is filled to capacity. At the Easter service in the Roman Catholic cathedral, one of the several masses was attended by over 2,000 worshippers. Other cities where Protestant churches have reopened and are welcoming congregations of 1,000 or more people are: Fuzhou (Foochow), Ningbo (Ning Po), Xiamen (Amoy), Hangzhou, and Guangzhou.

Moreover, church leaders are engaged in advanced stages of negotiations and preparations for resumption of public worship in such cities as Tianjin (Tientsin), Shenyang (formerly known as Mukden), Wuhan, Qingdao (Tsingtao), and Nanjing (Nanking). In Nanjing, there are many Christians meeting in house churches scattered throughout the city.

III

In detailing two cases of churches that have reopened, we are not implying that they are the only models being adopted. One fact we have discovered on this trip is that considerable diversity exists among China's various provinces—which in our context might be called "state's rights."

1. The East Mountain District Christian Church in Guangzhou held its first worship service on September 30, 1979. All of the churches in the entire province were closed during the Cultural Revolution. However, about twenty-five or thirty pastors and lay leaders continued meeting together in their homes. Partly to stay together as a group and partly to provide a means of employment, about 125 of the Protestant pastors organized a factory to manufacture equipment for classroom use. One of the church buildings was converted into the factory.

At the opening worship service, eight hundred people were in attendance. Even the pastors were surprised by the large turnout. Each Sunday thereafter, the number of worshippers has increased steadily. On December 2, 1979, over two thousand people jammed the facilities, filling the seats and sitting on newspapers on the floor. At one of the early services, the American consulate and his family were in attendance; they were the only non-Chinese persons present.

Surely two thousand people didn't just pop out of the woodwork.
What preparations were made in advance? What course did the resumption of activities take? Since the pastors had a continuing relationship
through work in the factory, an ongoing network had been established.
When it was decided to move forward with reopening, a committee of
pastors had to choose which building site would be most appropriate.
Many of the churches were canvassed, until the list was narrowed to the
four potential candidates with sufficiently large plant and facilities. They
included the United Church of China (UCC), Methodist, Christian Missionary Society (British), and the Dongshan Baptist Church. The Baptist
Church was selected, since its facilities best lent themselves to future
growth. In the complex of buildings was a large sanctuary, two high
schools, and a seminary for possible use in training future clergy and lay
leaders. An old board was found, scraped clean of earlier layers of paint,
and the new name, "Dongshan Tong," was painted to provide a bright
sign for the congregation.

Negotiations with government officials had been cordial and hospitable. In fact, not long after normalization, the Religious Affairs Bureau,
a national government agency (which itself was closed down during the
Cultural Revolution and resumed activities in January, 1979), actually
initiated the move to see if the church leaders were interested in resuming religious services. The government said it had spent $30,000 to re-
model and maintain the buildings, but since it has been using the buildings as the district office for the past thirty years without payment of
rent, they would call it even. So the congregation was able to recover its
ample facilities without additional building costs.

A problem facing the organizing committee was how to get the word
out to those interested, since church records of former members were destroyed or missing. It was decided to gather from memory all the names
of the members formerly associated with the Presbyterian Church (Sic
On Tong). About five hundred names were recalled and notices were
mailed to them. Of course, many by now were deceased and addresses
had changed. Those who were notified were requested to inform and
invite their friends to the opening service.

The organizing committee gathered a crew of volunteer workers to rebuild the chancel, build a cross, repaint the old pulpit, and collect the
necessary equipment. A large cross was mounted on the wall and flanked
by two red flags facing the congregation. A regular, rather traditional
Order of Service was mimeographed. What a surprise when eight hundred persons gathered to celebrate communion on September 30, 1979!

Four pastors are now serving this newly organized parish: Rev. Tong
Ma Tai (Baptist), Rev. Leung Bing Jue (Presbyterian), Rev. Leong Ney
Tau (Seventh Day Adventist—which holds a separate service on Satur-
days for two to three hundred people), and Rev. Fan Sou Ueun (Missionary Society).

As for the future, there is much optimism that the work will flourish.
Plans are already on the drawing boards for establishing additional par-
ishes. The site of the former Presbyterian Church has been selected for

the next opening. Its sanctuary has a capacity for 1,000. Already envisioned is a third site, for which there are three potential buildings from which to choose. A committee is at work to plan carefully and prudently, since they know full well that new foundations are being laid. This planning committee of pastors is meeting weekly for study, strategy, and prayer.

2. In Hangzhou, capital of the province of Zhejiang (Chekiang), we attended worship services unannounced at the Drum Tower Union Church. Formerly a Presbyterian church, it had been closed for the past thirteen years by the Cultural Revolution. Arriving ten minutes after the service began, we stood at the steps leading to a large and very crowded sanctuary. Every seat was taken and people were standing in the aisles and spilling over to the narthex and beyond to the street!

We were truly amazed and excited to find such a large body of worshippers inasmuch as our travel guide, when asked whether there is a Christian church in Hangzhou, remarked that he knew of one, but that only a few people go there!

Drum Tower Union Church held its reopening worship service on September 23, 1979, with one thousand persons in attendance. Two services are now conducted—the first one a 8:30 a.m. for twelve hundred worshippers, and the second one at 2:00 p.m. for eight hundred. The freshly painted sanctuary is simple and austere. A central pulpit is flanked by four chrysanthemum plants and a small cross is hung high on the wall. No pictures, paintings, or flags are visible. Two full-time and three part-time pastors serve the congregation. Both the senior pastor, Rev. S. B. Shen, and Rev. Mark Chen are Anglicans. Rev. Peter Tsai, who studied at Princeton and Drew seminaries in 1946–48, is Presbyterian, as is Rev. M. Y. Chen. Rev. Miss W. Y. Chi is Baptist.

During the years when the church was closed, its sanctuary was used as a warehouse for groceries. With the demise of the "Gang of Four" and the Cultural Revolution, the government's reactivated Bureau of Religious Affairs encouraged church leaders to resume public worship. Prior to reopening, small groups of scattered Christians continued meeting in homes for Bible study and prayer. The Bureau assisted in moving out the old tenants and has promised to assist in recovery of back rent for the use of church properties.

Preaching responsibilities are rotated among the five pastors, with each assuming the pulpit for a month at a time. This particular service began at 8:30 a.m. and concluded at 10:15 with the singing of the closing hymn, "What a Friend We Have in Jesus." Many worshippers brought bibles and followed as the scriptures were being read. American churchgoers should take heart that the sermon, which was based on the Gospel of John ("The Word Became Flesh . . ."), lasted for fifty-two minutes.

We were warmly received and were impressed by the fervent prayers uttered corporately and individually during the service, which was punctuated by frequent "amens." In meeting afterwards with the pastors, we were especially interested in the age breakdown of the membership. We noted quite a few college-age youth, teenagers, and primary school boys and girls. This question is significant, for it has been alleged that Christianity in China will disappear with the passing of the older generation of Christians. Such does not appear to be the case.

A study of the membership of 1,500 indicates that 65% are over 50 years of age, 25% are between 30 and 50, and 10% are under 30. This study also discovered that only 500 members had been baptized prior to the Cultural Revolution. Fully 1,000 are new believers or have come into the Christian fold during the time of the Cultural Revolution. Moreover, there is a youth choir of thirty to forty young people.

The pastors are encouraged by the zeal, commitment and contributions of the members. They foresee continuing growth. Negotiations are currently under way for the return of the facilities known as the "Pastor Chang Memorial Church," which has a seating capacity of 1,500. Since the Cultural Revolution, this site continues to be used by the Library for book storage. It is anticipated that this second church will be reopened in 1980. Long-range plans call for the opening of a Protestant congregation in each county of the province of Zhejiang.

IV

Since this is a time for self-development, it would, indeed, be a tragic mistake—tantamount to killing with kindness—for American churches and missionary boards to pour in personnel, funds, or materials for the churches in China. The best posture for American churches to assume is to respect the integrity of the Chinese churches, to allow them space and freedom for genuine self-development and self-growth.

As early as the 1920s, there were proponents of the principles of the "Three Self Movement": self-support, self-propagation of the Gospel, and self-administration. With the presence of so many well-meaning missionaries, who followed in the wake of the gunboats, there was virtually no way for the Three Self Movement principles to be implemented. After Liberation, the Three Self Movement was reaffirmed in September, 1950. Now the time has arrived for American churches to assiduously respect the Three Self Movement and to honor its intention. Let the Church of China be the Church of China!

The idea that the best way for Americans to help the Chinese churches is to leave them alone and simply pray for them, as they intend to pray for us, may be difficult advice for American Christians to hear and to pursue. We suspect that the mainline churches in America will understand and be sympathetic, whereas the more zealous evangelical groups will want to barge in with reckless abandon. To the latter, we would say, wait until the invitation has been issued, until the call to "come over to Macedonia" has been sounded, before you respond.

American Christians should be reassured that their counterparts in China are well aware of the imperative to share the Good News of the Gospel. Additional churches will be reopened as rapidly as is feasible.

An indigenous hymnal is being published in Shanghai, and a group of scholars, under the leadership of the Center for Religious Studies at Nanjing University, is publishing a revised version of the New Testament and the Psalms in simplified Chinese characters. This bible will be ready for distribution in 1980. So there is no need to flood the nation with hymnals or bibles produced from outside. That would be counterproductive.

May God grant all of us that special grace to be still and know that the Lord is at work in the Christian koinonia in China. At this juncture in history, all that is required of us are our prayers and our understanding.

Brief Bibliography

A. Doak Barnett and Edwin O. Reischauer, THE UNITED STATES AND CHINA. New York: Praeger Publishers, 1971 (Paper).

John K. Fairbank, THE UNITED STATES AND CHINA, 4th Edition, Cambridge: Harvard University Press, 1979.

Christopher Howe, CHINA'S ECONOMY. New York: Basic Books, 1978 (Paper).

Al Imfelt, CHINA AS A MODEL OF DEVELOPMENT. New York: Orbis Books, 1977 (Paper).

Stanley Karnow, MAO AND CHINA. New York: Viking Press, 1972.

Creighton Lacy, COMING HOME TO CHINA. Philadelphia: Westminster Press, 1978.

Qi Wen, CHINA: A GENERAL SURVEY. Peking: Foreign Language Press, 1979 (Paper).

Chester Ronnins, A MEMOIR OF CHINA IN REVOLUTION. New York: Pantheon Books, 1974.

Orville Schell, IN THE PEOPLE'S REPUBLIC. New York: Vintage Books, 1978 (Paper).

Franz Schurmann and Orville Schell, editors, IMPERIAL CHINA; REPUBLICAN CHINA; COMMUNIST CHINA (3-volume reader of source materials). New York: Vintage Books, 1967 (Paper).

Agnes Smedley, PORTRAITS OF CHINESE WOMEN IN REVOLUTION. New York) Feminist Press, 1976.

Edgar Snow, RED STAR OVER CHINA. New York: Grove Press, Bantam revised edition, 1978 (Paper).

Ross Terrill, 800,000,000. New York: Dell, 1978 (Paper).

Ross Terrill, editor, THE CHINA DIFFERENCE. New York: Harper Colophon, 1979 (Paper).

Raymond L. Whitehead, LOVE AND STRUGGLE IN MAO'S THOUGHT. New York: Orbis Books, 1977.

Franklin Woo, editor, CHINA NOTES. New York: National Council of Churches, issued quarterly.